WHY THE ROSARY, WHY NOW?

By Gretchen R. Crowe

**Our
Sunday
Visitor**

www.osv.com
Our Sunday Visitor Publishing Division
Our Sunday Visitor, Inc.
Huntington, Indiana 46750

Copyright © 2017 by Gretchen R. Crowe. Published 2017.

22 21 20 19 18 17   1 2 3 4 5 6 7 8 9

Our Sunday Visitor Publishing Division
Our Sunday Visitor, Inc.
200 Noll Plaza
Huntington, IN 46750
1-800-348-2440

ISBN: 978-1-68192-111-2 (Inventory No. T1841)
eISBN: 978-1-68192-135-8
LCCN: 2017930305

Cover design: Tyler Ottinger
Cover art: Shutterstock
Interior design: Dianne Nelson

PRINTED IN THE UNITED STATES OF AMERICA

About the Author

Gretchen R. Crowe is editor-in-chief of OSV Newsweekly, overseeing the publication of the only national Catholic weekly newspaper in the United States. In addition to planning and editing the print edition, she also oversees the content of OSVNews.com and Our Sunday Visitor's social media content. An award-winning writer and photographer, Crowe has been a member of the Catholic Press Association since 2005, and she serves on a liaison committee of the Catholic Press Association and Catholic News Service. She covered both the 2015 pastoral visit of Pope Francis and the 2008 pastoral visit of Pope Benedict XVI to the United States. Crowe is married to Michael Heinlein, and the couple is expecting their first child in May 2017.

Contents

Introduction

When I was a small child and would have difficulty going to sleep, I inevitably reached for my white rosary, given to me by my parents for my first Communion. Fingering the beads and reciting the repetitious prayers was soothing and calmed the thoughts that always seemed to swirl in my head at that time of night. When I contemplate the questions "Why the Rosary, why now?" I think of those moments that call out to us to reach to Mary for comfort, peace, and consolation. When we turn to her, she quiets our minds, calms our hearts, and focuses our thoughts where they should be more often: on her son.

Even as adults, there is much to be intimidated by in today's world: growing secularism and the disappearance of faith from the public square; the spread of evil and terrorism; war and violence; broken families; abounding distractions; a general lack of drive for holiness. But we know how to get to overcome these challenges today, just as people did one hundred years ago when Mary spoke to three shepherd children in Fátima, Portugal. In a series of apparitions, the Blessed Mother warned Jacinta, Francisco and Lucia of trials to come, and she strongly encouraged praying the Rosary for peace to reign in the world and in our hearts. This is not because the Rosary possesses magical powers, or because it is a talisman against evil. Rather, as the late Cardinal Francis E. George said at the conclusion of the Year of the Rosary in October 2003, the Rosary "brings us to the heart of the Gospel," to Jesus who is peace.

It's hard to believe that this one prayer can be the key to so many problems of such great magnitude. But indeed it is. The Rosary is our most secret of secret weapons, ready to be wielded against any challenge we face. Unfortunately, many Catholics take the Rosary for granted. We tend to purchase the strings of beads as souvenirs, stashing them here and there. Sometimes, when it is fashionable, we even wear them. Not nearly enough do we pray with them! But when we do, we discover that the Rosary is both the sword and the shield that helps us through the trials of everyday life.

Receiving the gifts of the Rosary to the fullest requires great perseverance and patience. We must enter into praying the Rosary with the same commitment and attention as we would enter into a conversation with a loved one. As Cardinal George said, "Relationships grow with familiarity, and praying the Rosary makes us familiar with the various dimensions of Christ's life." In order to get as much as possible from it, we must put as much as we can into it. Otherwise, our commitment will waver, indifference can take root, and our best efforts and intentions eventually will fade.

To that end, we must develop a strategy. Praying the Rosary daily should be planned, not left to chance. Make a routine out of it, whether undertaken while commuting, during a daily walk or run, or kneeling every night before bedtime. If you're feeling particularly motivated, make time to visit your parish's Blessed Sacrament chapel once a day to pray your Rosary in the presence of Jesus. Where you pray doesn't matter as much as consistency does. A routine will help trigger your brain, making you less likely to forget your commitment. The most important thing is to simply pray.

A commitment to praying a daily Rosary will put you in good company. The texts in this book were composed by men and women who experienced the power and many benefits of the Rosary in their own lifetimes. It is my hope that by reading the words of such wise and holy people, the reasons for praying the Rosary every day become not only undeniable but compelling.

World events may change, but one thing never does: the great grace available to us when we reach for our rosary beads and give our hearts to our Blessed Mother in prayer. So, Why the Rosary? Why Now? Because the Rosary is a pathway that leads us to the truth of Jesus Christ—a path that, as we will see in the following pages, has been trod steadily and faithfully by so many men and women of faith over the centuries.

CHAPTER ONE

To Break Through the Noise

I have a thing for audiobooks. Maybe it's the accents of the narrators, or the way I can enter into a story while convincing myself I am productively multitasking, or how they seem to calm and focus my overactive and seemingly ever-swirling thoughts. Whatever the reason, I own dozens of them, and I love to listen, and re-listen, to the stories. The more engrossed I am in them, however, the more I find that I tune out the world around me. Today's technology has made it possible to hop from activity to activity, all while being absorbed simultaneously by other things.

I'm not alone. For some of us, it's the lure of the Facebook or Twitter feed; for others, it's binge-watching television shows; for still more it's the never-ending texting conversation or Snapchat messaging. The noise is all around us, and it seems to never, ever end.

According to a Nielson report issued in June 2016, Americans spend more than ten hours a day looking at some type of screen, with smartphone usage alone up 60 percent from just a year prior. We tell ourselves we are being productive. We're using the tools at hand to stay connected with the world so we can better do our jobs or improve our knowledge. We're staying connected with loved ones. And those things are all partially true. But here's the real truth: When we are surrounded by constant noise, it becomes much more difficult to nurture relationships, including, and especially, our relationship with God.

This truth was expressed thoughtfully in a 1973 homily by Cardinal Albino Luciani, then archbishop of Venice, who would go on to be elected pontiff in 1978 and would take the name Pope John Paul I. The focus of Cardinal Luciani's homily was the Rosary and how it increasingly was being considered outdated, arcane, boring, and repetitious—in short, a thing of the past. But before he expanded on that theme, the cardinal first identified what he called a "crisis of prayer in general" facing the Church. "People are completely caught up in material interests; they think very little about their souls," he said. "And noise has invaded our existence."

If "Papa Luciani" identified the invasion of noise as a threat in 1973 Italy, what would he think of early twenty-first-century America? Indeed, in the early twenty-first century, Pope John Paul II wrote in his apostolic letter on the Rosary, *Rosarium Virginis Mariae,* that "one drawback of a society dominated by technology and the mass media is the fact that silence becomes increasingly difficult to achieve." And it's this lack of silence that helps lead to an atmosphere in which prayer, including the Rosary, is discarded.

Praying the Rosary, however, can help reverse this trend, even as it is threatened by it. By their very meditative nature, the prayers of the Rosary naturally enable one to break through the noise of everyday life and find silence. As Pope John Paul II wrote in his apostolic letter: "After the announcement of the mystery and the proclamation of the word, it is fitting to pause and focus one's attention for a suitable period of time on the mystery concerned, before moving into vocal prayer. A discovery of the importance of silence is one of the secrets of practicing contemplation and meditation" (31). In short, the Rosary not only benefits from silence, it helps foster it, and this is a lesson just as applicable today as it was 50 years ago.

When we speak of breaking through the noise, however, we must acknowledge the existence of internal noises that can be just as powerful as those that are external. These interior barriers to prayer often manifest themselves in the form of pride and self-centeredness. Here again we can look to the example of Cardinal Luciani and his episcopal motto: humility. On September 6, 1978, at one of the few General Audiences of his thirty-three-day pontificate, Pope John Paul I said: "I run the risk of making a blunder, but I will say it: The Lord loves humility so much that, sometimes, he permits serious sins. Why? In order that those who committed these sins may, after repenting, remain humble. One does not feel inclined to think oneself half a saint, half an angel, when one knows that one has committed serious faults. The Lord recommended it so much: be humble. Even if you have done great things, say: 'We are useless servants.' On the contrary, the tendency in all of us is rather the contrary: to show off. Lowly, lowly: this is the Christian virtue which concerns ourselves."

It is this lowliness that Cardinal Luciani refers to which can combat the internal noise that afflicts us. Many may consider the Rosary repetitious, boring, or what he calls a "poor prayer." But when we pray this simple prayer faithfully and with humility, the barriers of inner turmoil and distraction disappear. As we experience how the Rosary helps us break through the noise of our own pride and selfishness, we are better able to recognize how truly great the gift of the Rosary is and how it remains an essential tool to help us grow spiritually today.

As Pope Benedict XVI said in a 2008 address following the recitation of the most holy Rosary at the Basilica of St. Mary Major: "Today, together we confirm that the holy Rosary is not a pious practice banished to the past, like prayers of other times thought of with nostalgia. Instead, the Rosary is experiencing a new springtime. Without a doubt, this is one of the most eloquent signs of love that the young generation nourish for Jesus and his mother, Mary. In the current world, so dispersive, this prayer helps to put Christ at the center, as the Virgin did, who meditated within all that was said about her Son, and also what he did and said."

In the following homily, given against the backdrop of the aftermath of the Second Vatican Council and a changing Church, Cardinal Luciani gives a beautiful defense of the Rosary, one which we can still appreciate and take to heart today.

IS THE ROSARY OUTDATED?
Homily for the centenary of the feast of the Holy Rosary[1]
by Cardinal Albino Luciani (later Pope John Paul I)
October 7, 1973

What would happen during a meeting of Catholics if I were to invite the ladies and gentlemen to show what they had in their pockets or purses? I would certainly see a quantity of combs, pocket mirrors, tubes of lipstick, change purses, cigarette lighters, and other more or less useful little items. But how many rosaries? Years ago, I would have seen more of them.

In [Alessandro] Manzoni's house in Milan today, you can see his rosary beads hanging at the head of his bed: he said the Rosary habitually, and in his novel *The Betrothed*, Lucia [the heroine] pulled out her beads and said the Rosary at the most dramatic moments.[2]

Windthorst, a German statesman, was once invited by some friends who were non-practicing Catholics to show his rosary. It was a trick: they had removed his rosary from his left pocket beforehand. When Windthorst did not find it in the left one, he put his hand into the right and ended up looking good: He always carried a spare rosary! Christophe von Gluck, a great musician, used to withdraw for a few minutes during receptions at the Court of Vienna to say his Rosary. Blessed Contardo Ferrini, a university professor in Pavia, would invite his friends to say the Rosary when he was a guest in their home. St. Bernadette assured us that when Our Lady appeared to her, she had a rosary over her arm, asked her if she also had one, and invited her to say it, while the Virgin recommended the reciting of the Rosary to the three little shepherds at Fátima.

Why have I begun with this series of examples?

Because the Rosary is contested by some. They say: it is an infantile and superstitious prayer, not worthy of adult Christians. Or: it is a prayer that becomes automatic, reduced to a hasty, monotonous, and boring repetition of Hail Marys. Or: it's old-fashioned stuff; today there are better things: the reading of the Bible, for example, which is to the Rosary as the wheat is to the chaff!

On this subject, allow me to give a few impressions as a shepherd of souls.

A first impression: the crisis of the Rosary comes in second place. Today, in first place, there is a crisis of prayer in general. People are completely caught up in material interests; they think very little about their souls. And noise has invaded our existence. Macbeth would be able to repeat: "I have murdered sleep, I have murdered silence!"[3]

We have trouble finding a few little scraps of time for the inner life and the *dulcis sermoncinatio* or "sweet colloquy" with God. And it is a real loss. Donoso Cortes said, "Today the world is going badly because there are more battles than there are prayers." Communal liturgies, which are certainly a great good, are being developed: they are not enough, however; personal conversation with God is also necessary.

A second impression: When people talk about "adult Christians" in prayer, sometimes they exaggerate. Personally, when I speak alone with God and Our Lady, I prefer to feel like a child rather than an adult. The miter, the skullcap, and the ring disappear; I send the adult on vacation and the bishop too, with the staid, serious, and dignified behavior that go along with them, in order to abandon myself to the spontaneous tenderness that a child has for Mama and Papa. To be, at least for half an hour or so, as I am in reality, with my misery and the best of myself, to feel surfacing from the depths of my being the child I once was, a child who wants to laugh, chatter, and to love the Lord, and who sometimes feels the need to weep so that mercy may be shown him, helps me to pray. The Rosary, a simple and easy prayer, in turn, helps me to be a child, and I am not ashamed of it at all.

A third impression: I should not and do not want to think badly of anyone, but I confess that I have several times been tempted to conclude that this or that person thinks he is an adult just because he is acting like a judge, criticizing from on high. I feel like saying to him: "What do you mean, mature? When it comes to prayer, you are an adolescent in crisis, a disappointed and rebellious person, who has not yet gotten rid of the aggressiveness of the difficult age!" May God forgive me for my rash judgment! And now I come to the other objections.

Is the Rosary a repetitious prayer? Father [Charles] De Foucauld used to say, "Love is expressed in few words, always the same, and constantly repeated."

A woman who was traveling by train had put her baby to sleep in the baggage carrier.[4] When the little one awoke, he looked down from the carrier and saw his mother sitting in front of him watching over him. "Mama!" he said. And the other: "Darling!" And for a long while the dialogue between the two did not change: "Mama!" from above, "Darling!" from below. There was no need for other words.

Don't we have the Bible? Certainly, and it is a *quid summum*, but not everyone is prepared to read it or has time to. For those who do read it, it will also be useful for them at times, while traveling, on the street, and in times of particular need, to talk with Our Lady, if they believe that she is our mother and sister. If the reading of the Bible is just beginning to be appreciated as mere study, the mysteries of the Rosary, when meditated on and savored, are the Bible studied in depth, and made spiritual flesh and blood.

A boring prayer? It depends. It can be, instead, a prayer full of joy and happiness. If you know how to say it, the Rosary becomes a lifting of the eyes to Mary, which increases in intensity as you go on. It can also turn out to be a refrain that springs from the heart and calms the soul like a song.

A poor prayer, the Rosary? And what kind of prayer, then, would be "rich"? The Rosary is a series of Our Fathers, a prayer taught by Jesus, of Hail Marys, God's greeting of the Virgin through the Angel, of Glory Bes, the praise of the most Holy Trinity. Or would you like lofty theological ponderings instead? They wouldn't be suitable for the poor, the old, the humble, and the simple. The Rosary expresses faith without invented complications, without evasions, and without many words, it helps us to abandon ourselves to God and to accept suffering generously. God also makes use of theologians, but in distributing his grace, he makes use above all of the littleness of the humble and those who abandon themselves to his will.

There is another thing to be considered: The family should be the first school of piety and religious spirituality for the children. Religious teaching that comes from the parents, [Pope] Paul VI has said recently, is difficult, authorized, and irreplaceable. Difficult because of the climate of permissiveness and secularism that surrounds us; authorized, because it is part of the mission entrusted by God to parents; and irreplaceable, because it is in the most tender age that we develop the inclination towards and the habit of religious piety. The recitation of the Rosary, although in a shortened and adapted form in the evening by the parents together with their children, is a kind of domestic liturgy. The writer Louis Veuillot used to confess that the beginning of his return to God was the sight of the Rosary that he saw being said with faith by a Roman family.

With these convictions in my heart, it has been a consolation for me to hear of the initiative of the celebrations of the past few days. The Dominican Fathers, already so worthy because of their spreading of the Rosary in our city, and the "Gesuati," the parish of the Rosary par excellence, are planning the relaunching of this great and pious practice. Hoping that their work may be blessed by God, I have come to this liturgy as to a joyous religious festival.

Unfortunately, the joy is deeply disturbed by the rumblings of the ominous and senseless war that broke out yesterday in the Middle East. When, oh when, will men stop hating each other? When will they be willing to sacrifice their wretched dreams of an unstable national supremacy to the supreme and stable good of peace? When will we finally see an international body furnished with real powers for avoiding the outbreak of such disasters? We cannot help thinking at this moment with profound consternation of the impending harm to individuals, families, and entire nations; and of the anguish of so many of our brothers and sisters, who, for the most part, are helplessly suffering the consequences of decisions being taken at the top level of their nations. And the

Middle East is also a tinderbox. We must pray to the Lord not only that the war, which has unfortunately broken out, may remain limited, but that it may be quickly put under control and extinguished. In the Rosary we are accustomed to invoke Our Lady by her title of "Queen of Peace." Let us say to her fervently: *Regina pacis, ora pro nobis!*

NOTES

[1] Opera onium 6:199-202 (title by translator).

[2] *The Betrothed*, chapters 20, 21.

[3] Cf. *Macbeth*, II, ii, 37, 42.

[4] On Italian trains, the baggage carrier is a bag or net hanging above and in front of the seat.

CHAPTER TWO

For a Deeper Devotion to the Church

Archbishop Fulton J. Sheen, now declared venerable by the Church, had a way with words. Whether writing, speaking, or occasionally singing them, he captivated millions with his intellect and his passion. His vast theological knowledge, paired with his ability to clearly and succinctly explain the Church's teachings, has earned him a place among the preeminent evangelists of the twentieth century. Archbishop Sheen also had a deep devotion to the Blessed Virgin Mary, one that he worked tirelessly to share with others. In *The World's First Love: Mary, Mother of God*, first published in 1952, Archbishop Sheen described Mary as a "dream," a "mother," and a "spouse." In a talk titled "The Woman I Love," he indicated how Mary and the Church are intertwined because, he said, "as we discontinue our devotion to the Blessed Mother, there is always a decline in the love of the Church."

Such an observation certainly resonates for twenty-first-century Catholics in the United States who are witnessing a massive decline of love of the Church. A Pew Survey on "America's Changing Religious Landscape," released in May 2015, noted a significant drop in the number of American Catholics and a sharp increase in those who identified as "religiously unaffiliated" (also known as nones). Statistics have shown that one reason for these declining numbers is the growing discrepancy between the moral teachings of the Church and the evolution of our secular society. Developments in areas such as the legalization of same-sex marriage, abortion, and the increasing support for physician-assisted suicide—all of which are at odds with Church teaching—pit the Church more and more against the laws of the land. A lack of formation in the Faith of many baptized Catholics, a reality that was acknowledged and discussed openly at the 2014 and 2015 synods of bishops on the family in Rome, is another reason. As we experience this decline in the number of faithful, then, it follows that a decline also exists in the number of those who espouse a personal devotion to Mary—and through her to her Son.

According to Archbishop Sheen, praying with our Blessed Mother in the Rosary is the solution, and it can be the doorway through which we are led to love of Mary and, subsequently, to love of the Church. And this doorway is one that is open to all.

When seen in this light the following excerpt from *The World's First Love* is tremendously powerful. It outlines how the Rosary makes both Mary and Jesus accessible to all people, regardless of educational status or mental or physical health. In particular, Archbishop Sheen says, it is of benefit to several groups, in particular the worried, the intellectual and the unlearned, and the sick—situations in life to which each of us can relate.

After all, who among us has not suffered from worry? The last century alone gave us two world wars, multiple genocides, the continued destruction of the Middle East (what Pope Francis has called a "piecemeal" third world war), the development of a culture of death that includes abortion and euthanasia, the spread of terrorism at home and abroad, a growing aggressive secularism, and the increase in the persecution of Christians.

In America, it is becoming more difficult for men and women of faith, as well as religious organizations, to effectively defend their deeply held religious beliefs. While permitted in the privacy of houses of worship and family life, religious beliefs and practices increasingly are being challenged in the public square. This troubling development calls into question our very freedom of religion, one of the basic tenets of the U.S. Constitution. While societal changes like these are naturally cause for great concern, the Rosary can ease such fears. The prayer is, as Archbishop Sheen writes, a place where those who are distressed and wounded may find solace and strength. As you pray the Rosary, he says, "you will be surprised how you can climb out of your worries, bead by bead, up to the very throne of the Heart of Love Itself."

Who among us, too, has not experienced some moments of profound understanding and others where, quite differently, we feel as if we are drowning in our own inadequacy? The Rosary is the great equalizer, Archbishop Sheen writes, because it "is the meeting ground of the uneducated and the learned; the place where the simple love grows in knowledge and where the knowing mind grows in love." The prayer of the Rosary is, he says, a place "where intellectual elephants may bathe, and the simple birds may also sip."

Who among us has not been affected by illness—whether personally or through a loved one? The Rosary is there for each of us, ready and waiting to reconnect us with our Blessed Mother and, through her, the Church that her Son has given to us to help guide us to salvation.

It is impossible to end any kind of introduction to Archbishop Sheen, who served as the national director of the Pontifical Mission Societies from 1950 to 1966, without mentioning his love and affection for the poor. Though he does not name them specifically in the following excerpt, it was clear from his ministry that he believed the Rosary was a way to offer them special healing and consolation as well. In a February 1951 radio broadcast of "The Catholic Hour," Archbishop Sheen introduced the World Mission Rosary to "aid the Holy Father and his Society for the Propagation of the Faith by supplying him with practical support, as well as prayers, for the poor mission territories of the world." As he instructed, "We must pray, and not for ourselves, but for the world." The Rosary, he said, is a way to "embrace the world in prayer."

In a similar way, we are called to embrace the Rosary in prayer. Through it, wounds can be healed, faith can find rebirth, and a deeper love of the Church can be fostered. And we need this love now more than ever.

EXCERPT FROM *THE WORLD'S FIRST LOVE*
(Chapter 8: "Roses and Prayers")
by Fulton J. Sheen

No human who has ever sent roses to a friend in token of affection, or ever received them with gladness, will be alien to the story of prayer. And a deep instinct in humanity makes it associate roses with joy. Pagan peoples crowned their statues with roses as symbols of their own hearts. The faithful of the early Church substituted prayers for roses. In the days of the early martyrs—"early" because the Church has more martyrs today than it had in the first four centuries—as the young virgins marched over the sands of the Colosseum into the jaws of death, they clothed themselves in festive robes and wore on their heads a crown of roses, bedecked, fittingly, to meet the King of Kings in whose name they would die. The faithful, at night, would gather up these crowns of roses and say their prayers on them—one prayer for each rose. Far away in the desert of Egypt the anchorites and hermits were also counting their prayers, but in the form of little grains or pebbles strung together into a crown—a practice which Mohammed took for his Moslems. From this custom of offering spiritual bouquets arose a series of prayers known as the Rosary, for rosary means "crown of roses."

Not always the same prayers were said on the rosary. In the Eastern Church there was a Rosary called the Akathist (Akathistos), which is a liturgical hymn recited in any position except sitting. It combined a long series of invocations to the Mother of Our Lord, held together by a scene from the life of Our Lord on which one meditated while saying the prayers. In the Western Church, St. Brigid of Ireland used a Rosary made up of the Hail Mary and the Our Father. Finally, the Rosary as we know it today began to take shape.

From the earliest days, the Church asked its faithful to recite the one hundred and fifty Psalms of David. This custom still prevails among priests, who recite some of these Psalms every day. But it was not easy for anyone to memorize the one hundred and fifty Psalms. Then, too, before the invention of printing, it was difficult to procure a book. That is why certain important books like the Bible had to be chained like telephone books; otherwise people would have run off with them. Incidentally, this gave rise to the stupid lie that the Church would not allow anyone to read the Bible, because it was chained. The fact is, it was chained so people could read it. The telephone book is chained, too, but it is more consulted than any book in modern civilization!

The people who could not read the one hundred and fifty Psalms wanted to do something to make up for it. So, they substituted one hundred and fifty Hail Marys. They broke up these one hundred and fifty, in the manner of the Akathist, into fifteen decades, or series of ten. Each part was to be said while meditating on a different aspect of the life of Our Lord. To keep the decades separate, each one of them began with the Our Father and ended with the Doxology of Praise to the Trinity. St. Dominic, who died in 1221, received from the Blessed Mother the command to preach and to popularize this devotion for the good of souls, for conquest over evil, and for the prosperity of Holy Mother Church, and thus gave us the Rosary in its present classical form.

Practically all the prayers of the Rosary, as well as the details of the life of our Savior on which one meditates while saying it, are to be found in the Scriptures. The first part of the Hail Mary is nothing but the words of the angel to Mary; the next part, the words of Elizabeth to Mary on the occasion of her visit. The only exception is the last part of the Hail Mary—namely, "Holy Mary, Mother of God, pray for us sinners, now, and at the hour of our death. Amen." This was not introduced until the latter part of the Middle Ages. Since it seizes upon the two decisive moments of life: "now, and at the hour of our death," it suggests the spontaneous outcry of people in a great calamity. The Black Death, which ravaged all Europe and wiped out one-third of its population, prompted the faithful to cry out to the Mother of Our Lord to protect them, at a time when the present moment and death were almost one.

The Black Death has ended. But now the Red Death of Communism is sweeping the earth. In keeping with the spirit of adding something to this prayer when evil is intensified, I find it interesting that, when the Blessed Mother appeared at Fátima in 1917 because of the great decline in morals and the advent of godlessness, she asked that, after the "Glory be to the Father, Son, and Holy Spirit," we add, "O MY JESUS, forgive us our sins, save us from the fire of hell, lead all souls to heaven, especially those who are most in need of Thy mercy."

It is objected that there is much repetition in the Rosary because the Lord's Prayer and the Hail Mary are said so often; therefore, it is monotonous. That reminds me of a woman who came to see me one evening after instructions. She said:

"I would never become a Catholic. You say the same words in the Rosary over and over again, and anyone who repeats the same words is never sincere. I would never believe anyone who repeated his words, and neither would God." I asked her who the man was with her. She said he was her fiancé. I asked: "Does he love you?" "Certainly, he does." "But how do you know?" "He told me." "What did he say?" "He said, 'I love you.'" "When did he tell you last?" "About an hour ago." "Did he tell you before?" "Yes, last night." "What did he say?" "'I love you.'" "But never before?" "He tells me every night." I said: "Do not believe him. He is repeating; he is not sincere."

The beautiful truth is that there is no repetition in, "I love you." Because there is a new moment of time, another point in space, the words do not mean the same as they did at another time or space. A mother says to her son: "You are a good boy."

She may have said it ten thousand times before, but each time it means something different; the whole personality goes out to it anew, as a new historical circumstance summons forth a new outburst of affection. Love is never monotonous in the uniformity of its expression. The mind is infinitely variable in its language, but the heart is not. The heart of a man, in the face of the woman he loves, is too poor to translate the infinity of his affection into a different word. So, the heart takes one expression, "I love you," and in saying it over and over again, it never repeats. It is the only real news in the universe. That is what we do when we say the Rosary; we are saying to God, the Trinity, to the Incarnate Savior, to the Blessed Mother: "I love you, I love you, I love you." Each time it means something different because, at each decade, our mind is moving to a new demonstration of the Savior's love—for example, from the mystery of his love which willed to become one of us in his Incarnation, to the other mystery of love when he suffered for us, and on to the other mystery of his love where he intercedes for us before the heavenly Father. And who shall forget that Our Lord himself in the moment of his greatest agony repeated, three times within an hour, the same prayer?

The beauty of the Rosary is that it is not merely a vocal prayer. It is also a mental prayer. One sometimes hears a dramatic presentation in which, while the human voice is speaking, there is a background of beautiful music, giving force and dignity to the words. The Rosary is like that. While the prayer is being said, the heart is not hearing music, but it is meditating on the life of Christ all over again, applied to his own life and his own needs. As the wire holds the beads together, so meditation holds the prayers together. We often speak to people while our minds are thinking of something else. But in the Rosary we not only say prayers, we think them. Bethlehem, Galilee, Nazareth, Jerusalem, Golgotha, Calvary, Mount Olivet, heaven—all these move before our mind's eye as our lips pray. The stained-glass windows in a church invite the eye to dwell on thoughts about God. The Rosary invites our fingers, our lips, and our heart in one vast symphony of prayer, and for that reason is the greatest prayer ever composed by man. The Rosary has a special value to many groups: (1) the worried, (2) the intellectual and the unlearned, (3) the sick.

1. *The Worried.* Worry is a want of harmony between the mind and the body. Worried people invariably keep their

minds too busy and their hands too idle. God intended that the truths we have in our mind should work themselves out in action. "The Word became flesh"—such is the secret of a happy life. But in mental distress, the thousand and one thoughts find no order or solace within and no escape without. In order to overcome this mental indigestion, psychiatrists have taught soldiers suffering from war shock how to knit and do handicrafts, in order that the pent-up energy of their minds might flow out through the busy extremities of their fingers.

This is, indeed, helpful, but it is only a part of the cure. Worries and inner distress cannot be overcome by keeping the hands alone busy. There must be a contact with a new source of Divine Energy and the development of confidence and trust in a Person whose essence is love. Could worried souls be taught the love of the Good Shepherd who cares for the wayward sheep, so that they would put themselves into that new area of love—all their fears and anxieties would banish. But that is difficult. Concentration is impossible when the mind is troubled; thoughts run helter-skelter; a thousand and one images flood across the mind; distracted and wayward, the spiritual seems a long way off. The Rosary is the best therapy for these distraught, unhappy, fearful, and frustrated souls, precisely because it involves the simultaneous use of three powers: the physical, the vocal, and the spiritual, and in that order. The fingers, touching the beads, are reminded that these little counters are to be used for prayer. This is the physical suggestion of prayer. The lips move in unison with the fingers. This is a second or vocal suggestion of prayer. The Church, a wise psychologist, insists that the lips move while saying the Rosary, because she knows that the external rhythm of the body can create a rhythm of the soul. If the fingers and the lips keep at it, the spiritual will soon follow, and the prayer will eventually end in the heart.

The beads help the mind to concentrate. They are almost like the self-starter of a motor; after a few spits and spurts, the soul soon gets going. Every airplane must have a runway before it can fly. What the runway is to the airplane, that the Rosary beads are to prayer—the physical start to gain spiritual altitude. The very rhythm and sweet monotony induce a physical peace and quiet, and create an affective fixation on God. The physical and the mental work together if we give them a chance. Stronger minds can work from the mind outward; but worried minds have to work from the outside inward. With the spiritually trained, the soul leads the body; with most people, the body has to lead the soul. Little by little the worried, as they say the Rosary, see that all their worries stemmed from their egotism. No normal mind yet has ever been overcome by worries or fears who was faithful to the Rosary. You will be surprised how you can climb out of your worries, bead by bead, up to the very throne of the Heart of Love Itself.

2. *The Intellectual and the Unlearned.* The spiritual advantages which one derives from the Rosary depend upon two factors: first, the understanding that one has of the joys, sorrows, and glory in the life of Christ; and second, the fervor and love with which one prays. Because

the Rosary is both a mental and a vocal prayer, it is one where intellectual elephants may bathe, and the simple birds may also sip.

It happens that the simple often pray better than the learned, not because the intellect is prejudicial to prayer, but because, when it begets pride, it destroys the spirit of prayer. One always ought to love according to knowledge, for Wisdom and Love of the Trinity are equal. But as husbands who know they have good wives do not always love according to that knowledge, so too the philosopher does not always pray as he should, and thus his knowledge becomes sterile.

The Rosary is a great test of faith. What the Eucharist is in the order of sacraments, that the Rosary is in the order of sacramentals—the mystery and the test of faith—the touchstone by which the soul is judged in its humility. The mark of the Christian is the willingness to look for the Divine in the flesh of a babe in a crib, the continuing Christ under the appearance of bread on an altar, and a meditation and a prayer on a string of beads.

The more one descends to humility, the deeper becomes the faith. The Blessed Mother thanked her Divine Son because he had looked on her lowliness. The world starts with what is big, the spirit begins with the little, aye, with the trivial! The faith of the simple can surpass that of the learned, because the intellectual often ignore those humble means to devotion, such as medals, pilgrimages, statues, and rosaries. As the rich, in their snobbery, sneer at the poor, so the intelligentsia, in their sophistication, jeer at the lowly. One of the last acts of Our Lord was to wash the feet of his disciples, after which he told them that out of such humiliation true greatness is born.

When it comes to love, there is no difference between the intellectual and the simple. They resort to the same token of affection and the same delicate devices, such as the keeping of a flower, the treasuring of a handker-chief or a paper with a scribbled message. Love is the only equalizing force in the world; all differences are dissolved in the great democracy of affection. It is only when men cease to love that they begin to act differently. Then it is that they spurn the tiny little manifestations of affection which make love grow.

But if the simple and the intellectual love, in the human order, in the same way, then they should also love God in the Divine order, in the same way. The educated can explain love better than the simple, but they have no richer experience of it. The theologian may know more about the divinity of Christ, but he may not vitalize it in his life as well as the simple. As it is by the simple gesture of love that the wise man enters into the understanding of love, so it is by the simple acts of piety that the educat-ed also enter into the knowledge of God. The Rosary is the meeting ground of the uneducated and the learned; the place where the simple love grows in knowledge and where the knowing mind grows in love. As [Maurice] Maeterlinck has said, "The thinker continues to think justly only if he does not lose contact with those who do not think at all!"

3. *The Sick.* The third great value of the Rosary is for the sick. When fever mounts and the body aches, the mind cannot read; it hardly wants to be spoken to, but there is much in its heart it yearns to tell. Since the number of prayers one knows by heart is very limited, and their very repetition becomes wearisome in sickness, it is well for the sick to have a form of prayer in which the words focus or spearhead a meditation. As the magnifying glass catches and unites the scattered rays of the sun, so the Rosary brings together the otherwise dissipated thoughts of life in the sickroom: into the white and burning heat of Divine Love.

When a person is healthy, his eyes are, for the most part, looking to the earth; when he is flat on his back, his eyes look to heaven. Perhaps it is truer to say that heaven looks down on him. In such moments, when fever, agony, and pain make it hard to pray, the suggestion of prayer that comes from merely holding the Rosary is tremendous— or better still, caressing the crucifix at the end of it. Because our prayers are known by heart, the heart can now pour them out, and thus fulfill the scriptural injunction to "pray always." Prisoners of war during the last world war have told me how the Rosary enabled men to pray, almost continuously, for days before their death. The favorite mysteries then were generally the sorrowful ones, for by meditating on the suffering of Our Savior on the cross, men were inspired to unite their pains with him, so that, sharing in his cross, they might also share in his resurrection.

The Rosary is the book of the blind, where souls see and
there enact the greatest drama of love the world has ever
known; it is the book of the simple, which initiates them
into mysteries and knowledge more satisfying than the
education of other men; it is the book of the aged, whose
eyes close upon the shadow of this world, and open on
the substance of the next. The power of the Rosary is
beyond description. And here I am reciting concrete instances which I know. Young people, in danger of death
through accident, have had miraculous recoveries—a
mother, despaired of in childbirth, was saved with the
child—alcoholics became temperate—dissolute lives
became spiritualized—fallen-aways returned to the
Faith—the childless were blessed with a family—soldiers were preserved during battle—mental anxieties
were overcome—and pagans were converted. I know of
a Jew who, in World War I, was in a shell hole on the
Western Front with four Austrian soldiers. Shells had
been bursting on all sides. Suddenly, one shell killed his
four companions. He took a Rosary from the hands of
one of them and began to say it. He knew it by heart, for
he had heard others say it so often. At the end of the first
decade, he felt an inner warning to leave that shell hole.
He crawled through much mud and muck, and threw
himself into another. At that moment a shell hit the first
hole, where he had been lying. Four more times, exactly the same experience; four more warnings, and four
times his life was saved! He promised then to give his
life to Our Lord and to his Blessed Mother if he should
be saved. After the war, more sufferings came to him; his

family was burned by Hitler, but his promise lingered on. Recently, I baptized him—and the grateful soldier is now preparing to study for the priesthood.

All the idle moments of one's life can be sanctified, thanks to the Rosary. As we walk the streets, we pray with the Rosary hidden in our hand or in our pocket; driving an automobile, the little knobs under most steering wheels can serve as counters for the decades. While waiting to be served at a lunchroom, or waiting for a train, or in a store; or while playing dummy at bridge; or when conversation or a lecture lags—all these moments can be sanctified and made to serve inner peace, thanks to a prayer that enables one to pray at all times and under all circumstances. If you wish to convert anyone to the fullness of the knowledge of Our Lord and of his Mystical Body, then teach him the Rosary. One of two things will happen. Either he will stop saying the Rosary—or he will get the gift of faith.

CHAPTER THREE

To Strengthen Families

One of the first inklings I had that I was going to marry my husband was the first time we prayed the Rosary together. The familiar prayers, recited one after the other, so well-known by each of us, connected us in a way that I'd never experienced before. It was both peaceful and exhilarating—the beginning of a strong foundation based on a mutual love of Jesus Christ and his Blessed Mother.

That experience is one reason why the famous words of "Rosary priest" Father Patrick Peyton resonate so deeply with me: "The family that prays together stays together." This refrain was coined from Patrick Peyton's lived experience, starting at a young age. In his autobiography, *All for Her*, Father Peyton (1909-92) explains how the family Rosary was a priority in his home every evening. No matter how exhausted his parents or eight brothers and sisters were at the end of the day, patriarch John Peyton insisted that the family gather to thank the Blessed Mother for watching over them for another day.

As a striking contrast, Father Peyton describes what life was like on his first night away from home after securing a job nearby. Having been welcomed into temporary residency in a Catholic home, he initially felt comfortable with the familiar family setting. He was shocked, therefore, when his host ushered him off to bed without first calling the family together to pray the Rosary as his father would have. "I was thunderstruck, absolutely speechless at the realization that a Catholic home existed ... in which the people did not kneel together for family prayer," he wrote. "While I pretended to sleep, I prayed my own Rosary and felt the pangs of homesickness, the bitterness of being among people whose ways were different from my own, whose sense of values failed to measure up to what all my training and experience had told me was normal."

After a week, he finally admitted to his host how much it bothered him. "I don't know what I said, but it was my first sermon on family prayer, my first appeal to another Catholic to imitate the practice of my own family and reap the same rewards," he wrote.

Though he did not know it at the time, his appeal, however disjointed, was a success. The family soon after began praying the Rosary together every night.

This experience was clearly a pivotal moment for Peyton—one in which he realized that he could not and must not take the faith passed down to him by his parents for granted. And so it was this faith, personified in the Blessed Mother, to which he turned later in life when, during the course of his seminary studies, he fell gravely ill. The story of his return to health—his account of which follows—is the story of a miracle granted and a vocation confirmed. And it's an event that propelled Father Peyton, once ordained, to devote the rest of his life to spreading family prayer, particularly in the Rosary.

The following excerpts from the first four chapters of *All for Her* chronicle this portion of his life, beginning with his earliest days in Ireland and ending with his miraculous healing. Afterward, Father Peyton began the Family Rosary Crusade, making use of radio, film, outdoor signage, and more than two hundred sixty Rosary rallies on six continents to promote family prayer to millions of people.

Such an effort sounds particularly appealing in modern times when it seems that Catholic families are moving further away from the Church and from actively nurturing a spiritual life in general. A 2015 study by the Center for Applied Research in the Apostolate at Georgetown University, in conjunction with Holy Cross Family Ministries, which carries on the legacy of Father Peyton, indicated the following troubling statistics about the current state of family participation in a life of faith: Only 22 percent of Catholic families attend Mass weekly; 68 percent of Catholic parents have not enrolled their children in religious education; only 17 percent of parents who pray on their own also pray as a family; and only 13 percent of families pray together before meals.

In an effort to curb these and other challenging trends in family life, Church leaders today are putting an extra emphasis on a renewal of the family. When Pope Francis called for an extraordinary synod in 2014—only the third time in modern history for which such a step had been taken—its theme was "the pastoral challenges of the family in the context of evangelization." A second, ordinary synod on the family was held a year later, the focus of which was "the vocation and mission of the family in the Church and in the contemporary world." Catholics were encouraged to pray for the success of these meetings, particularly using the Rosary.

In Pope Francis' apostolic exhortation that followed, *Amoris Laetitia* ("The Joy of Love"), the pope echoed Father Peyton's call to family prayer and the role that Church leaders play in promoting it. "We pastors have to encourage families to grow in faith," he wrote. "This means encouraging frequent confession, spiritual direction and occasional retreats. It also means encouraging family prayer during the week, since 'the family that prays together stays together.' When visiting our people's homes, we should gather all the members of the family and briefly pray for one another, placing the family in the Lord's hands. It is also helpful to encourage each of the spouses to find time for prayer alone with God, since each has his or her secret crosses to bear. Why shouldn't we tell God our troubles and ask him to grant us the healing and help we need to remain faithful?" (227).

Of course, encouraging family spirituality has been a focus of other pontiffs, as well, specifically when it comes to encouraging the praying of the Rosary. In the conclusion of *Rosarium Virginis Mariae*, St. John Paul II reiterated that the Rosary is "and always has been, a prayer of and for the family." "At one time this prayer was particularly dear to Christian families, and it certainly brought them closer together," he wrote. "It is important not to lose this precious inheritance. We need to return to the practice of family prayer and prayer for families, continuing to use the Rosary."

And Pope St. Pius X (r. 1903-14) is credited with saying, "The Rosary is the most beautiful and the most rich in graces of all prayers; it is the prayer that touches most the Heart of the Mother of God ... and if you wish peace to reign in your homes, recite the family Rosary."

Such is our mission today—to build a strong foundation of faith guided by our Mother Mary and the immortal reminder of Father Peyton that "the family that prays together stays together." The Rosary is the key to fostering such prayer and, in short, to strengthening the family.

EXCERPTS FROM *ALL FOR HER*
Autobiography of Father Patrick Peyton

Carracastle in the first decades of this century was a straggly little village of thatched one-story cabins set in a fold of the foothills of the Ox Mountains, a few miles from the Atlantic Ocean in the bleak western part of County Mayo, Ireland.... I was born in one of those cabins in 1909, and it was my home for the first nineteen years of my life. I always think that this was a great grace, not because it was a thatched cabin, but because it was a home of prayer. Starting on their wedding day my parents knelt each evening before the hearth to say together the family Rosary, that God and Mary might protect and bless their home and fill it with the laughter of children. God heard that daily prayer. He blessed my parents with a large family. They, for their part, expressed their gratitude in the way they knew best. In all the years of their married life they never once failed to gather the family every evening for the recitation of Mary's centuries-old prayer....

The dominant quality of my father, the one that gave a unity to all the rest, was his great spirit of faith. This, of course, is characteristic of the culture in which I was raised. The language is sprinkled with expressions of piety. Heaven and earth are intertwined in the mind and the imagination. We lived among holy wells, the memories of saints who had labored in the same fields, the hiding places of persecuted priests, and the rocks on which they had celebrated the Mass.

All of this was embodied in my father to a high degree. In his presence, one felt uplifted, almost like being in church. I don't mean that he preached to us. What impressed me was the way he lived and the way he prayed, especially when each evening we all knelt together to say the Rosary. If there was one inflexible rule in our home, it was that every one of us had to participate in the family Rosary led by my father. It didn't matter how hard or how long the day's work—digging potatoes, cutting turf, or repairing a road. Often one or another would drop to sleep on his knees. But he was always brought back into the prayer, kindly but firmly. It was the entire family praising God, asking him through his Mother to protect it, to guide it to the destiny he had intended for it. That nightly scene constitutes my earliest memory and the most abiding. From it I derive the entire pattern and purpose of my existence.

After being formed through prayer in the family home, young Patrick discerned a vocation to the priesthood, but his aspirations were put off repeatedly as he moved from Ireland to the United States, finished school, and began working. Eventually, he enrolled in Moreau Seminary within Notre Dame University and, having discerned a vocation to mission work, entered the Holy Cross's Foreign Missionary Seminary (the Bengalese), a house of study in Washington, D.C., for theologians preparing for missionary work. "I had reached the home stretch," he wrote in his autobiography of the long process. "The frequently denied goal of the priesthood was finally in sight.... I was full of energy, and I was determined to extract the maximum value from these last four years, so that I might emerge as fully qualified as lay in my power." Unfortunately, it was not quite that simple.

In this way a year went by with the speed of a single day. I was well into the second when indications of possibly serious trouble began to develop in October 1938. From the early part of that year I had been finding it harder to drive myself. The grueling pace was taking its toll, but I had refused to read the signs. I just forged ahead, a glutton for work, both physical and mental, with no rest or no willingness to rest.

So it continued until one day in October I noticed a speck of blood on my handkerchief. At first I thought nothing of it. As a boy, I had frequent nosebleedings [sic], and I told myself it was simply a recurrence. Several times, however, the symptom was repeated when I coughed. I had to face the fact that I was spitting up blood. To anyone from Ireland that could mean only one thing in those days, the disease whose name was seldom mentioned but which everyone knew. Tuberculosis was endemic, and its progress through lingering years of idleness and discomfort to early death was taken for granted, once it was diagnosed....

For three months I lay on the flat of my back in Providence Hospital. There was no question about the diagnosis. I had tuberculosis all right.… In May, it was decided to transfer me to the infirmary at Notre Dame, then located in the building which earlier had been my novitiate house. I had recovered sufficiently to permit continuation of the treatment at Healthwin Sanitarium, about three miles away. This sanitarium specialized in treating tuberculosis victims, and my superior hoped that the specialists and the change of air would hasten my recovery.…

The progress of my illness was getting me down. The doctors at Healthwin were continuing the treatment started in Washington, intended to collapse the affected lung. I went out there once a week for an injection of air into the pulmonary sac. Things would go well for a while, and then I'd have a setback; another period of encouragement, and another letdown. Even prayer no longer brought me any happiness. In fact it was an effort to pray at all.… I could not concentrate on anything. So I lay on the bed all through those burning summer months and stared at the ceiling day after day, week after week, month after month, knowing all the time that I was getting worse instead of better.…

In September, I had another setback that scared me. When I reported it at my weekly visit at Healthwin, Dr. John A. Mart said it was time to make a full evaluation of the treatment. He ordered X rays and blood tests. A week later I returned full of anxiety for the verdict. It was just about as gloomy as it could be: "My colleagues and I have studied the X rays and samples. We have reviewed the entire history of the case. I am sorry to report that the treatment is a failure."

"And is there nothing else you can try?" I asked dejectedly. "There is a possibility, but it is a possibility of desperation," he answered. "My colleagues and myself would be prepared to undertake an operation. The pneumotherapy is not working, and we are now convinced it will not work for you. The only alternative is to remove several ribs and break several others. It will involve three major operations, and the effect will be to make your shoulder blade fall in, giving your lung the rest that is essential for recovery."

"It's a desperate mutilation of a man's body," I said. "It would leave him handicapped for life, even if it worked."

"I know," he said, "and that is why my colleagues and I want you to think the thing over and make your own decision. You are a man dedicated to God. Your choice now is to put yourself in our hands and trust to our efforts, or to write us off and put your trust in God and in prayer."…

"This is finally the summit of Calvary," I told myself. My heart was torn. At best, even if the operation were successful, I was going to lose another whole year. I might easily be forced to abandon altogether my dream of the priesthood. Still I didn't want to yield to despair. I tried to think of myself as being really on Calvary, really willing to share in Christ's sufferings, and to accept my own fate as coming from the hands of God.

The next day I reported the situation to my superior at the infirmary, Father Thomas Irving, and he was all in favor of the operation. More than that, he wanted to get the business over before the ice and snow of winter set in. I was ready to obey, but my spirit still revolted. One point I could not get out of my mind was that three medical doctors, one Jewish and the others Protestants, had challenged my belief that my fate was in the hands of God. I knew that they were good doctors and honorable men. In their own minds they must have little hope of success, if they were leaving it to me to choose. But what an agonizing choice they offered me!...

The news spread quickly across the campus, and it brought Father Cornelius Hagerty running to me. As he stood in the doorway of my room that night in late October, a distant memory flooded back, filled me with joy, and put me in a state of receptivity for what he was going to say to me. I recalled the first time I had ever set eyes on him. It was, I believe, my first year in the community, and I was out for a walk at Notre Dame one afternoon with several of my companions. "That's Father Hagerty," one of them said, pointing to a priest in the distance. Although we did not exchange a word, the mere sight of him left a mark on me: his serenity, his dignity, his peaceful face. All our subsequent relations had confirmed that first impression. Here was a man who would never wear a false face. He would say what he believed regardless of the consequences. I welcomed him to my room with open arms.

Father Cornelius and I have more than once tried to reconstruct what exactly passed between us that night. The precise words have vanished forever, and it may well be that I read more into them than he intended by them. If I did, I believe that we are both now agreed that this was providential. For he forced me to face squarely the issue that the doctors had presented to me: Was my faith a sham or a reality? He handed me the correct answer, and all I can do is to thank

God and Mary for the rest of my life that I had the grace to accept it.

About certain parts of the conversation I am quite clear. He may not even have known about the choice the doctors had offered me, though he obviously did know that they had given me bad news. But what he said fitted [*sic*] perfectly into my situation and gave me the key to my decision. "You have the faith, Pat," he said, "but you're not using it. You brought it with you from Ireland. Your mother gave it to you, just as her mother had given it to her." He dwelt on that point, recalling a passage in which St. Paul describes how the faith is transmitted from mother to son.

Then he explained to me how meaningful prayer to our Blessed Mother would be, if only I used the faith I possessed. "Our Lady will be as good as you think she is," he said. "If you think she is a fifty percenter, that is what she will be; if you think she is a hundred percenter, she will be for you a hundred percenter. No one of us ever does as much as he is capable of doing. We always fall short, stopping on the near side of our total effort."

It was startling to be addressed in such words, but not nearly as startling as what he said next. "Even Our Lord and Our Lady do not do as much as they could do," he added, "but the reason is that we think they are not able. We limit them by the extent of our faith." Then he made me another wonderful statement: "I will begin a novena of Masses for you tomorrow, and that's the greatest thing on earth. It is not just some holy man or some holy woman praying for you for nine days. It is Jesus Christ praying to his Father for you. And that is a power infinitely greater than any power on earth."

He went on talking for a long time in this vein, restoring my confidence in the goodness and mercy of God, insisting that the way to reach God was through the intercession of Mary. As I listened, I felt that he was building a bridge for me over the chasm that spelt the difference between theory and reality, that he was leading me across that bridge so that I could see Mary, could walk with her, talk to her, realize that she was a real person who would listen, love, respond. I will not say that I really saw Mary for the first time while he talked, but I know I saw her with a new clarity and intensity, so that I could say in my heart: "Mother, I believe that you are alive, that you are real, that you are a woman, that you have eyes, a face, a smile, a memory, an intelligence, a heart. You have a mother and father of your own. You have a son, who is truly God, who loves you, who will deny you nothing you ask."

Many beautiful things Father Hagerty said. But what really captivated me was the way he summed up his entire thinking in three brief statements. "Mary is omnipotent in the power of her prayer," he said. "Mary is omnipotent in the power of her intercession with her Son. Mary can do anything God can do." Then he went on to explain the meaning of these three statements. "The difference is not in what God can do and what Mary can do. The difference is in the way they do it. God wills something and it happens. Mary prays to him for something and he does it. He will never say no to her."

The total impact of what Father Hagerty said was to add a new dimension to the love I already had for the Mother of

God. To a greater extent than ever before, he helped me to realize how human she is, how approachable, how sensitive to our needs, so that she could never be haughty or turn her back when we call her. I saw how strong my own position was in dealing with her. All those years, from the time I was able to lisp the prayers, I had joined with my family in praising her and paying tribute to her. It was like a man who had paid an insurance over the years on his house. Now the house was burning down and he could come and claim on his insurance.

I knew what I had to do. There would be no operations. I would put my trust in God, and I would approach him through his Mother and mine. She would cure me....

Father Hagerty's visit was about October 25, and during the following days my peace of mind and my confidence grew. I prayed continuously to Mary to cure me, and it was on Halloween, the eve of All Saints, that I knew that she had decided to do just that. I was eating my supper in bed, and the radio was playing some Irish tunes, transmitted from London. Just then the oppression and the depression and the darkness were swept from my soul, to be replaced by a lightness, a freedom, and a hope. I had been up and down many times, but this was different. The fog had finally lifted.

I was due to go to Healthwin the following Monday, November 6, for my weekly treatment. I decided to say nothing to anyone until the doctor found out for themselves. But interiorly I was at peace.... The first procedure, each time I went to the sanitarium, was to put me under the fluoroscope to determine how much gas should be pumped into the pulmonary sac. Two of the doctors were present, and the moment they took the first look, one of them beckoned the other to withdraw to a corner where they could talk without being overheard. They didn't have to tell me. I knew that something wonderful had happened. Here were the men who a few weeks earlier had told me it was hopeless, and now they were back out of the corner, turning me this way and that, checking, examining, making notes.

"How is the fluid?" I asked. The presence of fluid in the sac was a complication which prevented the collapsing of the lung. "It's not all gone," one of them said, "but it's going." ... A week later, on November 13, I was back again at Healthwin. "How is the fluid now?" I asked with mounting confidence. "It's all gone," they said. "There's not a trace of it left."

"In that case," I said, "why don't you discharge me as cured? You must realize what happened. You challenged me to put my trust in God, and that is what I did. It was Mary, the Mother of God, who heard my prayers. She does not do things by half. She wants me to go back to my studies, and you mustn't stand in my way."

They were very polite. They agreed that they had no way to account for the sudden improvement. But they were also quite firm. "Now we must continue the treatment," they said. "You must wait until the end of the six-month period from your last full examination. Until that study of your condition is completed, you must follow the regime we have laid down."

That same evening I had a visit from a young student priest, Father Richard Sullivan, who many years later was to be my provincial. "I am going to offer a novena of Masses for you," he told me, "to end on the feast of the Presentation of Our Lady, November 21." Lying in my bed each morning during those nine days, I joined in spirit with Father Sullivan, and I looked forward with anticipation to Mary's feast. I was not disappointed. The evening of November 20, I knelt for a long time before the picture of our Blessed Mother in my room, and I then took Lourdes water from a bottle and rubbed it on my chest. In the morning the sputum cup which is the constant companion of the victim of tuberculosis was clean. I had not coughed up a single taste of poison from my lungs all night, nor did I ever again use that sputum cup. On Our Lady's day I was allowed up for a while. I was weak and pale, but I wanted to be a member of the community again, and it was a great happiness to go to the recreation room and chat with the priests.

I was more determined than ever to force the issue with the doctors at Healthwin, but they were equally adamant that I would have to wait out the full six months before repeating the major examination which I was confident would give me a clean bill of health. My dilemma was quickly resolved by Father Christopher J. O'Toole, who subsequently served a term as superior general of Holy Cross. He had been ordained a few years earlier and had gone for further studies to Louvain University, Belgium. With the outbreak of war in Europe in September 1939, he had been brought back home and made assistant to Father Irving at the infirmary while awaiting a new assignment. Day by day he had followed my rapid improvement, and he now made arrangements to have Dr. James McMeel of South Bend examine me independently. The X rays and other tests were made at St. Joseph's Hospital, South Bend, on December 5. Two days later Dr. McMeel called Brother Michael. "Tell Pat Peyton," he said, "that he can get up for Mass tomorrow."

Tomorrow was the feast of the Immaculate Conception of Mary. It was a Mass I had always attended with love, but never before did the Scripture readings affect me as they did that day. The tone was set by the opening words of the Introit: "I will heartily rejoice in the Lord, in my God is the joy of my soul, for he has clothed me with a robe of salvation" (Is 61:10). And when the priests came to the final words of the epistle, I thought it was more than my heart could contain: "He who finds me finds life, and wins favor from the Lord" (Prv 8:35). It was indeed true. Finding Mary, I had found life and had been clothed with a robe of salvation.

Armed with this assurance, I pestered the Healthwin doctors until they finally agreed to move up the examination. They were still understandably skeptical, and they went about their task methodically and thoroughly. They completed their examinations and tests on January 15, 1940, and a few days later they mailed me the verdict. I shall never forget the moment it reached me. For a long time I held the letter in my hand, not daring to open it. I felt like the man in the dock as the jury files back into the court to announce its findings. I knew that I was cured, just as the man in the dock may know that he is innocent, but that doesn't mean that the verdict will go in his favor. My terror was that they would be overcautious, that they would insist on keeping me in bed, force me to lose another year. Finally, however, I prayed and summoned my faith. I tore the envelope open with shaking hands. Mary had not deceived me. "After discussing your situation at our staff conference," the letter read, "we came to the conclusion that you could safely take eleven hours a week. It is important that you get as much rest as possible, and if at any time new symptoms develop, you should contact us immediately. Pneumothorax will be continued with refills every two weeks."... I was lifted to heaven in delight by the news, yet it also frightened me. This was Mary's own doing, and she would bear the responsibility. "Mary, I hope I will never disgrace you," I cried aloud, my heart full of gratitude that I was free to continue toward my goal.

After completing his studies at Holy Cross College, on the campus of The Catholic University of America in Washington, D.C., Father Peyton was ordained June 15, 1941, at the University of Notre Dame. And when the ordaining bishop commenced the laying on of hands, Father Peyton's mind was flooded with thoughts about his long and difficult journey.

I did not hesitate when I heard my name; yet when the bishop's hands touched my head, I felt almost crushed by the weight of the burden they were placing on me. Henceforth I would always have to carry that burden, not only in time but through all eternity, or as the Book put it, "even in heaven, even in hell." The bishop told me that Christ's yoke was sweet and his burden light, but how could such a one as I carry it worthily? All my past life welled up in a single vision before my eye. Here was I, a farm boy from a Mayo village, a road worker, a general handyman, a helper on a steam shovel, an obstinate and often ungrateful son. Now I was being transformed into another Christ. I was being given power to make Christ present in the Christian community under the appearances of bread and wine. I was being authorized to forgive sin in his name. I was being commissioned to preach his word, so that those who heard me heard him. I could enroll new recruits in the ranks of the people of God by pouring on their heads the saving waters of baptism. I could strengthen the dying for their final journey by anointing them with the holy oils of the Sacrament of the Sick.

It was a terrifying experience but a supremely salutary one. For when the vision passed, what remained was that I was now by ordination another Christ and that consequently Christ's Mother was, more than ever before, my mother. If in the past she had behaved with such delicacy toward me, what could I not now expect from her, now that I was another Christ, the very fruit of her womb? The thought filled me with consolation and exaltation beyond all describing. If I had the heavens in my hand at that moment, I'd have given them right to her. At Notre Dame that day, I gave my heart and soul in love to Mary. I promised her all the merit of my priesthood until death. The merit and the glory of every action I would ever perform would be hers and hers alone.

CHAPTER FOUR

For an Increase in Christian Discipleship

I will never forget the young woman. She was kneeling, eyes shut, head bent, arms extended, her face adorned with a beautiful smile. Her words were spoken aloud, as if talking to a beloved: "Jesus, I love you. I love you." It was the first time my college-aged self heard words like that spoken as a prayer. The young woman's witness, shared unselfconsciously among a group of her peers, evidenced what seemed to be a deep, personal relationship with Christ—one that I wanted very badly.

It's likely I'm not alone. No doubt each of us somewhere along the path of life has come across someone of deep prayer or faith whom we greatly admire and perhaps even envy. Each of us, in fact, is called by Jesus into this type of close, loving relationship with him—and from that intimacy he commissions us forth to serve others. "Do you love me?" he asks Peter in the twenty-first chapter of the Gospel of John. If so, then "feed my sheep."

The best way that we can live out this command is by
participating in the sacramental life of the Church: to worship the Lord at Mass and to receive the grace of the sacraments. But we also are called to cultivate a personal relationship with God which involves a daily commitment to a life
of discipleship. Such is our calling at all times, but particularly today, when witnesses of faith sadly are becoming more
scarce. But how do we do this?

In the book *Forming Intentional Disciples: The Path to
Knowing and Following Jesus*, Sherry Weddell outlines five
stages of spiritual growth that typify the experience of conversion include:

- developing initial trust through a "positive association"
  with Jesus, the Church, or someone else they identify as
  Christian;
- developing a spiritual curiosity, in which the individual
  desires to know more about Jesus or Christianity;
- being open to personal and spiritual change;
- spiritual seeking, in which one actively seeks to know
  God;
- and, finally, intentional discipleship, where one con-
  sciously commits to following Christ, including making
  the changes to one's life that reflect that commitment.

Each of these stages is important for those aspiring to
live lives of discipleship today. But none of them would
be possible, however, without first encountering Christ, a
theme that both Pope Benedict XVI and Pope Francis have
mentioned repeatedly. As Pope Benedict said in a 2007
speech, "The person's and the human community's evange-

lization depends absolutely on the existence or lack thereof of the encounter with Jesus Christ." And in his apostolic exhortation *Evangelii Gaudium* ("The Joy of the Gospel"), Pope Francis invited "all Christians, everywhere, at this very moment, to a renewed personal encounter with Jesus Christ, or at least an openness to letting him encounter them" (3).

If, then, we are to become evangelized disciples of Jesus Christ, to do our best to meet him face to face, there is no better model to whom we should look than the person who encountered him first: his mother. Mary, after all, lived with her eyes fixed on Christ, treasuring all the moments of his life and, as St. Luke explains, pondering them in her heart (see Lk 2:19; 2:51). With her "yes" to the Angel Gabriel, and ultimately to God, at the Annunciation, Mary becomes the first Christian, the first person, to accept Jesus Christ into her life and heart—even into her own body.

When we pray the Rosary, we use the mysteries to meditate on different moments in Jesus' life, all through the lens of his holy mother. As Pope St. John Paul II writes in *Rosarium Virginis Mariae*, the first two chapters of which appear next, "the Rosary is one of the traditional paths of Christian prayer directed to the contemplation of Christ's face" (18). This contemplation leads us to a personal encounter with Jesus Christ, the first step toward Christian discipleship. Recounting what Pope Paul VI wrote in *Marialis Cultus*, St. John Paul points out that the "quiet rhythm" and "lingering pace" of the Rosary fosters meditation on Jesus' life "as seen through the eyes of her who was closest to the Lord," thereby finding "unfathomable riches" (12).

St. John Paul identifies Mary in the primary way she is meant to be seen—as one who points to Christ. "Do whatever he tells you," she says to the servers at the wedding in Cana (see Jn 2:5). In *Rosarium Virginis Mariae*, he adds to the treasure-trove of "unfathomable riches" found in the Rosary by proposing an additional five mysteries of the prayer, the Mysteries of Light. By meditating on all twenty mysteries of the Rosary, through Mary's perspective, we are brought into a deeper understanding of both his human and divine natures. This deeper understanding is what sets us on the path to becoming disciples of Jesus Christ and to living our lives accordingly.

There is a startling dearth of Christian discipleship in the world today, mostly because it is not easy to deny yourself, take up your cross, and follow him (see Mt 16:24). Discipleship calls us to set aside ego, selfishness, and pride, and to instead prioritize others. In today's society, where we are conditioned now more than ever that we may have whatever we want whenever we want it, the path of self-sacrifice seems radically countercultural. Yet this is the life to which Jesus calls each of us. Mary and the Rosary can help us get there.

In 1999, the U.S. bishops published "Our Hearts Were Burning Within Us," a pastoral plan for adult education in the United States. In it, they stated that the "adult disciple" of Christ enjoys many fruits: those of the Holy Spirit (love, joy, peace, patience, kindness, generosity, faithfulness, gentleness, and self-control); the fruits of justice and compassion; and the fruit of evangelization. "Mature faith is open to the action and power of God's Spirit and cannot remain idle or unproductive," they wrote. "Where the Spirit is active, faith is fruitful" (60).

The goal of mature discipleship, an active spirit, and a fruitful faith, then, is why encountering Jesus in the Rosary is so critical. This is what leads us to be able to kneel down, extend our arms in adoration and supplication, and say: "Jesus, I love you. I love you. What do you want of me?"

EXCERPTS FROM ROSARIUM VIRGINIS MARIAE
by Pope St. John Paul II

CHAPTER 1
CONTEMPLATING CHRIST WITH MARY

A face radiant as the sun

9. "And he was transfigured before them, and his face shone like the sun" (Mt 17:2). The Gospel scene of Christ's transfiguration, in which the three apostles Peter, James, and John appear entranced by the beauty of the Redeemer, can be seen as an icon of Christian contemplation. To look upon the face of Christ, to recognize its mystery amid the daily events and the sufferings of his human life, and then to grasp the divine splendor definitively revealed in the risen Lord, seated in glory at the right hand of the Father: this is the task of every follower of Christ and therefore the task of each one of us. In contemplating Christ's face we become open to receiving the mystery of Trinitarian life, experiencing ever anew the love of the Father and delighting in the joy of the Holy Spirit. St. Paul's words can then be applied to us: "Beholding the glory of the Lord, we are being changed into his likeness, from one degree of glo-

ry to another; for this comes from the Lord who is the Spirit" (2 Cor 3:18).

Mary, model of contemplation

10. The contemplation of Christ has an incomparable model in Mary. In a unique way the face of the Son belongs to Mary. It was in her womb that Christ was formed, receiving from her a human resemblance which points to an even greater spiritual closeness. No one has ever devoted himself to the contemplation of the face of Christ as faithfully as Mary. The eyes of her heart already turned to him at the Annunciation, when she conceived him by the power of the Holy Spirit. In the months that followed she began to sense his presence and to picture his features. When at last she gave birth to him in Bethlehem, her eyes were able to gaze tenderly on the face of her Son, as she "wrapped him in swaddling cloths, and laid him in a manger" (Lk 2:7).

Thereafter Mary's gaze, ever filled with adoration and wonder, would never leave him. At times it would be a questioning look, as in the episode of the finding in the Temple: "Son, why have you treated us so?" (Lk 2:48); it would always be a penetrating gaze, one capable of deeply understanding Jesus, even to the point of perceiving his hidden feelings and anticipating his decisions, as at Cana (cf. Jn 2:5). At other times it would be a look of sorrow, especially beneath the Cross, where her vision would still be that of a mother giving birth, for Mary not only shared the passion and death of her Son, she also received the new son given to her in the beloved disciple (cf. Jn 19:26-27). On the morning of Easter hers would be a gaze radiant with the joy of the Resurrection, and, finally, on the day of Pentecost, a gaze afire with the outpouring of the Spirit (cf. Acts 1:14).

Mary's memories

11. Mary lived with her eyes fixed on Christ, treasuring his every word: "She kept all these things, pondering them in her heart" (Lk 2:19; cf. 2:51). The memories of Jesus, impressed upon her heart, were always with her, leading her to reflect on the various moments of her life at her Son's side. In a way those memories were to be the "rosary" which she recited uninterruptedly throughout her earthly life.

Even now, amid the joyful songs of the heavenly Jerusalem, the reasons for her thanksgiving and praise remain unchanged. They inspire her maternal concern for the pilgrim Church, in which she continues to relate her personal account of the Gospel. Mary constantly sets before the faithful the "mysteries" of her Son, with the desire that the contemplation of those mysteries will release all their saving power. In the recitation of the Rosary, the Christian community enters into contact with the memories and the contemplative gaze of Mary.

The Rosary, a contemplative prayer

12. The Rosary, precisely because it starts with Mary's own experience, is an exquisitely contemplative prayer.

Without this contemplative dimension, it would lose its meaning, as Pope Paul VI clearly pointed out: "Without contemplation, the Rosary is a body without a soul, and its recitation runs the risk of becoming a mechanical repetition of formulas, in violation of the admonition of Christ: 'In praying do not heap up empty phrases as the Gentiles do; for they think they will be heard for their many words' (Mt 6:7). By its nature the recitation of the Rosary calls for a quiet rhythm and a lingering pace, helping the individual to meditate on the mysteries of the Lord's life as seen through the eyes of her who was closest to the Lord. In this way the unfathomable riches of these mysteries are disclosed."

It is worth pausing to consider this profound insight of Paul VI, in order to bring out certain aspects of the Rosary which show that it is really a form of Christocentric contemplation.

Remembering Christ with Mary

13. Mary's contemplation is above all a remembering. We need to understand this word in the biblical sense of remembrance (*zakar*) as a making present of the works brought about by God in the history of salvation. The Bible is an account of saving events culminating in Christ himself. These events not only belong to "yesterday"; they are also part of the "today" of salvation. This making present comes about above all in the Liturgy: what God accomplished centuries ago did not only affect the direct witnesses of those events; it continues to affect people in every age with its gift of grace. To some

extent this is also true of every other devout approach to those events: to "remember" them in a spirit of faith and love is to be open to the grace which Christ won for us by the mysteries of his life, death, and resurrection.

Consequently, while it must be reaffirmed with the Second Vatican Council that the Liturgy, as the exercise of the priestly office of Christ and an act of public worship, is "the summit to which the activity of the Church is directed and the font from which all its power flows," it is also necessary to recall that the spiritual life "is not limited solely to participation in the liturgy. Christians, while they are called to prayer in common, must also go to their own rooms to pray to their Father in secret (cf. Mt 6:6); indeed, according to the teaching of the apostle, they must pray without ceasing (cf. 1 Thes 5:17)." The Rosary, in its own particular way, is part of this varied panorama of "ceaseless" prayer. If the Liturgy, as the activity of Christ and the Church, is a saving action par excellence, the Rosary, too, as a "meditation" with Mary on Christ, is a salutary contemplation. By immersing us in the mysteries of the Redeemer's life, it ensures that what he has done and what the liturgy makes present is profoundly assimilated and shapes our existence.

Learning Christ from Mary

14. Christ is the supreme Teacher, the revealer and the one revealed. It is not just a question of learning what he taught but of "learning him." In this regard could we have any better teacher than Mary? From the divine standpoint, the Spirit is the interior teacher who leads us

to the full truth of Christ (cf. Jn 14:26; 15:26; 16:13). But among creatures no one knows Christ better than Mary; no one can introduce us to a profound knowledge of his mystery better than his Mother.

The first of the "signs" worked by Jesus—the changing of water into wine at the marriage in Cana—clearly presents Mary in the guise of a teacher, as she urges the servants to do what Jesus commands (cf. Jn 2:5). We can imagine that she would have done likewise for the disciples after Jesus' ascension, when she joined them in awaiting the Holy Spirit and supported them in their first mission. Contemplating the scenes of the Rosary in union with Mary is a means of learning from her to "read" Christ, to discover his secrets, and to understand his message.

This school of Mary is all the more effective if we consider that she teaches by obtaining for us in abundance the gifts of the Holy Spirit, even as she offers us the incomparable example of her own "pilgrimage of faith." As we contemplate each mystery of her Son's life, she invites us to do as she did at the Annunciation: to ask humbly the questions which open us to the light, in order to end with the obedience of faith: "Behold I am the handmaid of the Lord; be it done to me according to your word" (Lk 1:38).

Being conformed to Christ with Mary

15. Christian spirituality is distinguished by the disciple's commitment to become conformed ever more fully to his Master (cf. Rom 8:29; Phil 3:10,12). The outpouring

of the Holy Spirit in baptism grafts the believer like a branch onto the vine which is Christ (cf. Jn 15:5) and makes him a member of Christ's mystical Body (cf. 1 Cor 12:12; Rom 12:5). This initial unity, however, calls for a growing assimilation which will increasingly shape the conduct of the disciple in accordance with the "mind" of Christ: "Have this mind among yourselves, which was in Christ Jesus" (Phil 2:5). In the words of the apostle, we are called "to put on the Lord Jesus Christ" (cf. Rom 13:14; Gal 3:27).

In the spiritual journey of the Rosary, based on the constant contemplation—in Mary's company—of the face of Christ, this demanding ideal of being conformed to him is pursued through an association which could be described in terms of friendship. We are thereby enabled to enter naturally into Christ's life and as it were to share his deepest feelings. In this regard Blessed Bartolo Longo has written: "Just as two friends, frequently in each other's company, tend to develop similar habits, so too, by holding familiar converse with Jesus and the Blessed Virgin, by meditating on the mysteries of the Rosary and by living the same life in holy Communion, we can become, to the extent of our lowliness, similar to them and can learn from these supreme models a life of humility, poverty, hiddenness, patience, and perfection."

In this process of being conformed to Christ in the Rosary, we entrust ourselves in a special way to the maternal care of the Blessed Virgin. She who is both the Mother of Christ and a member of the Church, indeed her "preeminent and altogether singular member," is at the same time the "Mother of the Church." As such, she continually brings to birth children for the mystical Body of her Son. She does so through her intercession, imploring upon them the inexhaustible outpouring of the Spirit. Mary is the perfect icon of the motherhood of the Church.

The Rosary mystically transports us to Mary's side as she is busy watching over the human growth of Christ in the home of Nazareth. This enables her to train us and to mold us with the same care, until Christ is "fully formed" in us (cf. Gal 4:19). This role of Mary, totally grounded in that of Christ and radically subordinated to it, "in no way obscures or diminishes the unique mediation of Christ, but rather shows its power." This is the luminous principle expressed by the Second Vatican Council which I have so *powerfully experienced in my own life and have made the basis of my episcopal motto: Totus Tuus.* The motto is, of course, inspired by the teaching of St. Louis Marie Grignion de Montfort, who explained in the following words Mary's role in the process of our configuration to Christ: "Our entire perfection consists in being conformed, united, and consecrated to Jesus Christ. Hence the most perfect of all devotions is undoubtedly that which conforms, unites, and consecrates us most perfectly to Jesus Christ. Now, since Mary is of all creatures the one most conformed to Jesus Christ, it follows that among all devotions that which most consecrates and conforms a soul to Our Lord is devotion to Mary, his Holy Mother, and that the more a soul is consecrated to her the more will it be consecrated to Jesus Christ." Never as in the Rosary do the life of Jesus and that of Mary appear so deeply joined. Mary lives only in Christ and for Christ!

Praying to Christ with Mary

16. Jesus invited us to turn to God with insistence and the confidence that we will be heard: "Ask, and it will be given to you; seek, and you will find; knock, and it will be opened to you" (Mt 7:7). The basis for this power of prayer is the goodness of the Father, but also the mediation of Christ himself (cf. 1 Jn 2:1) and the working of the Holy Spirit who "intercedes for us" according to the will of God (cf. Rom 8:26-27). For "we do not know how to pray as we ought" (Rom 8:26), and at times we are not heard "because we ask wrongly" (cf. Jas 4:2-3).

In support of the prayer which Christ and the Spirit cause to rise in our hearts, Mary intervenes with her maternal intercession. "The prayer of the Church is sustained by the prayer of Mary." If Jesus, the one Mediator, is the Way of our prayer, then Mary, his purest and most transparent reflection, shows us the Way. "Beginning with Mary's unique cooperation with the working of the Holy Spirit, the Churches developed their prayer to the Holy Mother of God, centering it on the person of Christ manifested in his mysteries." At the wedding of Cana the Gospel clearly shows the power of Mary's intercession as she makes known to Jesus the needs of others: "They have no wine" (Jn 2:3).

The Rosary is both meditation and supplication. Insistent prayer to the Mother of God is based on confidence that her maternal intercession can obtain all things from the heart of her Son. She is "all-powerful by grace," to use the bold expression, which needs to be properly understood, of Blessed Bartolo Longo in his Supplication to Our Lady. [*Supplication to the Queen of the Holy Rosary* was composed by Blessed Bartolo Longo in 1883 in response to an appeal of Pope Leo XIII.] This is a conviction which, beginning with the Gospel, has grown ever more firm in the experience of the Christian people. The supreme poet Dante expresses it marvelously in the lines sung by St. Bernard: "Lady, thou art so great and so powerful, that whoever desires grace yet does not turn to thee, would have his desire fly without wings" [*Divina Commedia*, Paradiso XXXIII, 13-15].

When in the Rosary we plead with Mary, the sanctuary of the Holy Spirit (cf. Lk 1:35), she intercedes for us before the Father who filled her with grace and before the Son born of her womb, praying with us and for us.

Proclaiming Christ with Mary

17. The Rosary is also a path of proclamation and increasing knowledge, in which the mystery of Christ is presented again and again at different levels of the Christian experience. Its form is that of a prayerful and contemplative presentation, capable of forming Christians according to the heart of Christ. When the recitation of the Rosary combines all the elements needed for an effective meditation, especially in its communal celebration in parish-

es and shrines, it can present a significant catechetical opportunity which pastors should use to advantage. In this way too Our Lady of the Rosary continues her work of proclaiming Christ. The history of the Rosary shows how this prayer was used in particular by the Dominicans at a difficult time for the Church due to the spread of heresy. Today we are facing new challenges. Why should we not once more have recourse to the Rosary, with the same faith as those who have gone before us? The Rosary retains all its power and continues to be a valuable pastoral resource for every good evangelizer.

CHAPTER 2
MYSTERIES OF CHRIST—
MYSTERIES OF HIS MOTHER

The Rosary, "a compendium of the Gospel"

18. The only way to approach the contemplation of Christ's face is by listening in the Spirit to the Father's voice, since "no one knows the Son except the Father" (Mt 11:27). In the region of Caesarea Philippi, Jesus responded to Peter's confession of faith by indicating the source of that clear intuition of his identity: "Flesh and blood has not revealed this to you, but my Father who is in heaven" (Mt 16:17). What is needed, then, is a revelation from above. In order to receive that revelation, attentive listening is indispensable: "Only the experience of silence and prayer offers the proper setting for the growth and development of a true, faithful, and consistent knowledge of that mystery."

The Rosary is one of the traditional paths of Christian prayer directed to the contemplation of Christ's face. Pope Paul VI described it in these words: "As a Gospel prayer, centered on the mystery of the redemptive Incarnation, the Rosary is a prayer with a clearly Christological orientation. Its most characteristic element, in fact, the litanylike succession of Hail Marys, becomes in itself an unceasing praise of Christ, who is the ultimate object both of the Angel's announcement and of the greeting of the mother of John the Baptist: 'Blessed is the fruit of your womb' (Lk 1:42). We would go further and say that the succession of Hail Marys constitutes the warp on which is woven the contemplation of the mysteries. The Jesus that each Hail Mary recalls is the same Jesus whom the succession of mysteries proposes to us now as the Son of God, now as the Son of the Virgin."

A proposed addition to the traditional pattern

19. Of the many mysteries of Christ's life, only a few are indicated by the Rosary in the form that has become generally established with the seal of the Church's approval. The selection was determined by the origin of the prayer, which was based on the number 150, the number of the Psalms in the Psalter.

I believe, however, that to bring out fully the Christological depth of the Rosary it would be suitable to make an addition to the traditional pattern which, while left to the freedom of individuals and communities, could broaden it to include the mysteries of Christ's public ministry between his baptism and his passion. In the course of those mysteries we contemplate important aspects of the person of Christ as the definitive revelation of God. Declared the beloved Son of the Father at the Baptism in the Jordan, Christ is the one who announces the coming of the Kingdom, bears witness to it in his works, and proclaims its demands. It is during the years of his public ministry that the mystery of Christ is most evidently a mystery of light: "While I am in the world, I am the light of the world" (Jn 9:5).

Consequently, for the Rosary to become more fully a "compendium of the Gospel," it is fitting to add, following reflection on the Incarnation and the hidden life of Christ (the Joyful Mysteries), and before focusing on the sufferings of his passion (the Sorrowful Mysteries) and the triumph of his resurrection (the Glorious Mysteries), a meditation on certain particularly significant moments in his public ministry (the Mysteries of Light). This addition of these new mysteries, without prejudice to any essential aspect of the prayer's traditional format, is meant to give it fresh life and to enkindle renewed interest in the Rosary's place within Christian spirituality as a true doorway to the depths of the Heart of Christ, ocean of joy and of light, of suffering and of glory.

The Joyful Mysteries

20. The first five decades, the "joyful mysteries," are marked by the joy radiating from the event of the Incarnation. This is clear from the very first mystery, the Annunciation, where Gabriel's greeting to the Virgin of Nazareth is linked to an invitation to messianic joy: "Rejoice, Mary."

The whole of salvation history, in some sense the entire history of the world, has led up to this greeting. If it is the Father's plan to unite all things in Christ (cf. Eph 1:10), then the whole of the universe is in some way touched by the divine favor with which the Father looks upon Mary and makes her the Mother of his Son. The whole of humanity, in turn, is embraced by the fiat with which she readily agrees to the will of God.

Exultation is the keynote of the encounter with Elizabeth, where the sound of Mary's voice and the presence of Christ in her womb cause John to "leap for joy" (cf. Lk 1:44). Gladness also fills the scene in Bethlehem, when the birth of the divine Child, the Savior of the world, is announced by the song of the angels and proclaimed to the shepherds as "news of great joy" (Lk 2:10).

The final two mysteries, while preserving this climate of joy, already point to the drama yet to come. The Presentation in the Temple not only expresses the joy of the Child's consecration and the ecstasy of the aged Simeon; it also records the prophecy that Christ will be a "sign of contradiction" for Israel and that a sword will pierce his mother's heart (cf. Lk 2:34-35). Joy mixed with drama marks the fifth mystery, the finding of the twelve-year-old Jesus in the Temple. Here he appears in his divine wisdom as he listens and raises questions, already in effect one who "teaches." The revelation of his mystery as the Son wholly dedicated to his Father's affairs proclaims the radical nature of the Gospel, in which even the closest of human relationships are challenged by the absolute demands of the Kingdom. Mary and Joseph, fearful and anxious, "did not understand" his words (Lk 2:50).

To meditate upon the "joyful" mysteries, then, is to enter into the ultimate causes and the deepest meaning of Christian joy. It is to focus on the realism of the mystery of the Incarnation and on the obscure foreshadowing of the mystery of the saving Passion. Mary leads us to discover the secret of Christian joy, reminding us that Christianity is, first and foremost, *euangelion*, "good news," which has as its heart and its whole content the person of Jesus Christ, the Word made flesh, the one Savior of the world.

The Mysteries of Light

21. Moving on from the infancy and the hidden life in Nazareth to the public life of Jesus, our contemplation brings us to those mysteries which may be called in a special way "mysteries of light." Certainly the whole mystery of Christ is a mystery of light. He is the "light of the world" (Jn 8:12). Yet this truth emerges in a special way during the years of his public life, when he proclaims the Gospel of the Kingdom. In proposing to the Christian community five significant moments—"luminous" mysteries—during this phase of Christ's life, I think that the following can be fittingly singled out: (1) his Baptism in the Jordan, (2) his self-manifestation at the wedding of Cana, (3) his proclamation of the kingdom of God, with his call to conversion, (4) his Transfiguration, and, finally, (5) his institution of the Eucharist as the sacramental expression of the Paschal Mystery.

Each of these mysteries is a revelation of the Kingdom now present in the very person of Jesus. The Baptism in the Jordan is first of all a mystery of light. Here, as Christ descends into the waters, the innocent one who became "sin" for our sake (cf. 2 Cor 5:21), the heavens open wide and the voice of the Father declares him the beloved Son (cf. Mt 3:17 and parallels), while the Spirit descends on him to invest him with the mission which he is to carry out. Another mystery of light is the first of the signs, given at Cana (cf. Jn 2:1-12), when Christ changes water into wine and opens the hearts of the disciples to faith, thanks to the intervention of Mary, the first among believers. Another mystery of light is the preaching by which Jesus proclaims the coming of the kingdom of God, calls to conversion (cf. Mk 1:15) and forgives the sins of all who draw near to him in humble trust (cf. Mk 2:3-13; Lk 7:47-48): the inauguration of that ministry of mercy which he continues to exercise until the end of the world, particularly through the Sacrament of Reconciliation which he has entrusted to his Church (cf. Jn 20:22-23). The mystery of light par excellence is the Transfiguration, traditionally believed to have taken place on Mount Tabor. The glory of the Godhead shines forth from the face of Christ as the Father commands the astonished apostles to "listen to him" (cf. Lk 9:35 and parallels) and to prepare to experience with him the agony of the Passion, so as to come with him to the joy of the Resurrection and a life transfigured by the Holy Spirit. A final mystery of light is the institution of the Eucharist, in which Christ offers his body and blood as food under the signs of bread and wine, and testifies "to the end" his love for humanity (Jn 13:1), for whose salvation he will offer himself in sacrifice.

In these mysteries, apart from the miracle at Cana, the presence of Mary remains in the background. The Gospels make only the briefest reference to her occasional presence at one moment or other during the preaching of Jesus (cf. Mk 3:31—5:46; Jn 2:12), and they give no indication that she was present at the Last Supper and the institution of the Eucharist. Yet the role she assumed at Cana in some way accompanies Christ throughout his ministry. The revelation made directly by the Father at the Baptism in the Jordan and echoed by John the Baptist is placed upon Mary's lips at Cana, and it becomes the great maternal counsel which Mary addresses to the Church of every age: "Do whatever he tells you" (Jn 2:5). This counsel is a fitting introduction to the words and signs of Christ's public ministry, and it forms the Marian foundation of all the "mysteries of light."

The Sorrowful Mysteries

22. The Gospels give great prominence to the sorrowful mysteries of Christ. From the beginning, Christian piety, especially during the Lenten devotion of the Way of the Cross, has focused on the individual moments of the Passion, realizing that here is found the culmination of the revelation of God's love and the source of our salvation. The Rosary selects certain moments from the Passion, inviting the faithful to contemplate them in their hearts and to relive them. The sequence of meditations begins with Gethsemane, where Christ experiences a

moment of great anguish before the will of the Father, against which the weakness of the flesh would be tempted to rebel. There Jesus encounters all the temptations and confronts all the sins of humanity, in order to say to the Father, "Not my will but yours be done" (Lk 22:42 and parallels). This "Yes" of Christ reverses the "No" of our first parents in the Garden of Eden. And the cost of this faithfulness to the Father's will is made clear in the following mysteries; by his scourging, his crowning with thorns, his carrying the cross, and his death on the cross, the Lord is cast into the most abject suffering: *Ecce homo!*

This abject suffering reveals not only the love of God but also the meaning of man himself.

Ecce homo: the meaning, origin, and fulfilment of man is to be found in Christ, the God who humbles himself out of love "even unto death, death on a cross" (Phil 2:8). The sorrowful mysteries help the believer to relive the death of Jesus, to stand at the foot of the cross beside Mary, to enter with her into the depths of God's love for man, and to experience all its life-giving power.

The Glorious Mysteries

23. "The contemplation of Christ's face cannot stop at the image of the Crucified One. He is the Risen One!" The Rosary has always expressed this knowledge born of faith and invited the believer to pass beyond the darkness of the Passion in order to gaze upon Christ's glory in the Resurrection and Ascension. Contemplating the

Risen One, Christians rediscover the reasons for their own faith (cf. 1 Cor 15:14) and relive the joy not only of those to whom Christ appeared—the apostles, Mary Magdalene, and the disciples on the road to Emmaus— but also the joy of Mary, who must have had an equally intense experience of the new life of her glorified Son. In the Ascension, Christ was raised in glory to the right hand of the Father, while Mary herself would be raised to that same glory in the Assumption, enjoying beforehand, by a unique privilege, the destiny reserved for all the just at the resurrection of the dead. Crowned in glory—as she appears in the last glorious mystery—Mary shines forth as Queen of the Angels and Saints, the anticipation and the supreme realization of the eschatological state of the Church.

At the center of this unfolding sequence of the glory of the Son and the Mother, the Rosary sets before us the third glorious mystery, Pentecost, which reveals the face of the Church as a family gathered together with Mary, enlivened by the powerful outpouring of the Spirit and ready for the mission of evangelization. The contemplation of this scene, like that of the other glorious mysteries, ought to lead the faithful to an ever greater appreciation of their new life in Christ, lived in the heart of the Church, a life of which the scene of Pentecost itself is the great "icon." The glorious mysteries thus lead the faithful to greater hope for the eschatological goal towards which they journey as members of the pilgrim People of God in history. This can only impel them to bear courageous witness to that "good news" which gives meaning to their entire existence.

From "mysteries" to the "Mystery": Mary's way

24. The cycles of meditation proposed by the Holy Rosary are by no means exhaustive, but they do bring to mind what is essential, and they awaken in the soul a thirst for a knowledge of Christ continually nourished by the pure source of the Gospel. Every individual event in the life of Christ, as narrated by the Evangelists, is resplendent with the Mystery that surpasses all understanding (cf. Eph 3:19): the Mystery of the Word made flesh, in whom "all the fullness of God dwells bodily" (Col 2:9). For this reason the Catechism of the Catholic Church places great emphasis on the mysteries of Christ, pointing out that "everything in the life of Jesus is a sign of his Mystery" [515]. The *"duc in altum"* of the Church of the third millennium will be determined by the ability of Christians to enter into the "perfect knowledge of God's mystery, of Christ, in whom are hidden all the treasures of wisdom and knowledge" (Col 2:2-3). The Letter to the Ephesians makes this heartfelt prayer for all the baptized: "May Christ dwell in your hearts through faith, so that you, being rooted and grounded in love, may have power ... to know the love of Christ which surpasses knowledge, that you may be filled with all the fullness of God" (3:17-19).

The Rosary is at the service of this ideal; it offers the "secret" which leads easily to a profound and inward knowledge of Christ. We might call it Mary's way. It is the way of the example of the Virgin of Nazareth, a woman of faith, of silence, of attentive listening. It is also the way of a Marian devotion inspired by knowledge of the inseparable bond between Christ and his Blessed Mother: the mysteries of Christ are also in some sense the mysteries of his Mother, even when they do not involve her directly, for she lives from him and through him. By making our own the words of the Angel Gabriel and St. Elizabeth contained in the Hail Mary, we find ourselves constantly drawn to seek out afresh in Mary, in her arms and in her heart, the "blessed fruit of her womb" (cf. Lk 1:42).

Mystery of Christ, mystery of man

25. In my testimony of 1978 mentioned above [No. 2 of this document, not reprinted here], where I described the Rosary as my favorite prayer, I used an idea to which I would like to return. I said then that "the simple prayer of the Rosary marks the rhythm of human life."

In the light of what has been said so far on the mysteries of Christ, it is not difficult to go deeper into this anthropological significance of the Rosary, which is far deeper than may appear at first sight. Anyone who contemplates Christ through the various stages of his life cannot fail to perceive in him the truth about man. This is the great affirmation of the Second Vatican Council which I have so often discussed in my own teaching since the encyclical letter *Redemptor Hominis*: "it is only in the mystery of the Word made flesh that the mystery of man is seen in its true light." The Rosary helps to open up the way to this light. Following in the path of Christ, in whom man's path is "recapitulated," revealed, and redeemed, believers come face to face with the image of the true man. Contemplating Christ's birth, they learn of the sanctity of life; seeing the household of Nazareth, they learn the original truth of the family according to God's plan; listening to the Master in the mysteries of his public ministry, they find the light which leads them to enter the kingdom of God; and following him on the way to Calvary, they learn the meaning of salvific suffering. Finally, contemplating Christ and his Blessed Mother in glory, they see the goal towards which each of us is called, if we allow ourselves to be healed and transformed by the Holy Spirit. It could be said that each mystery of the Rosary, carefully meditated, sheds light on the mystery of man.

At the same time, it becomes natural to bring to this encounter with the sacred humanity of the Redeemer all the problems, anxieties, labors, and endeavors which go to make up our lives. "Cast your burden on the Lord and he will sustain you" (Ps 55:23). To pray the Rosary is to hand over our burdens to the merciful hearts of Christ and his Mother. Twenty-five years later, thinking back over the difficulties which have also been part of my exercise of the Petrine ministry, I feel the need to say once more, as a warm invitation to everyone to experience it personally: The Rosary does indeed "mark the rhythm of human life," bringing it into harmony with the "rhythm" of God's own life, in the joyful communion of the Holy Trinity, our life's destiny and deepest longing.

CHAPTER FIVE

For Peace in the World

One of my favorite Bible verses comes from St. Paul's letter to the Christian community at Philippi in which he counsels them on everyday living: "Have no anxiety at all, but in everything, by prayer and petition, with thanksgiving, make your requests known to God. Then the peace of God that surpasses all understanding will guard your hearts and minds in Christ Jesus" (Phil 4:6-7).

That sometimes-desperate search for peace—especially amid a tumultuous world where peace remains elusive on a global scale, as well as in our communities and sometimes even our families—is something that can resonate with each of God's faithful as we seek to do his will. But if there's one guarantee about the Rosary, it's that we can and should use it as a tool to help pray for peace. We know this because Our Lady herself told us—or rather she told three shepherd children in Fátima, Portugal, in 1917—when she said, "Continue to say the Rosary every day in honor of Our Lady of the Rosary, to obtain the peace of the world and the end of the war, because only she can obtain it."

When Mary appeared at Fátima, this message of world peace was particularly poignant. The world was embroiled in World War I, which by its end claimed the lives of 38 million people. Since then, the world has endured a second world war, in which another 60 million people died, and other deadly conflicts have followed.

One of the most profound disruptions to peace in modern times was the dropping of atomic bombs on Hiroshima and Nagasaki in Japan. While the bombs brought a swift conclusion to World War II, the peace it gained was not without great cost. "My God, what have we done?" were the words of Captain Robert A. Lewis, copilot of the *Enola Gay*, which dropped "Little Boy" onto Hiroshima on August 6, 1945.

Remarkably, four Jesuit priests—Hugo Lassalle, Hubert Schiffer, Wilhelm Kleinsorge, and Hubert Cieslik—survived the attack despite being inside a church rectory located just eight blocks from the epicenter. Not only did they survive—and with only minor wounds—but none of them suffered any lasting effects from the radiation. They credited the Blessed Virgin Mary for their safety, explaining, "We were living the message of Fátima, and we prayed the Rosary every day." The result, they added, is that "prayer is more powerful than the atom bomb." What a sentiment!

The text that follows is the story of these priests, as related by Father Schiffer, in which he stresses the importance of praying for peace and invites others to join him.

"Our Blessed Mother's rosary is a bond which unites the heart strings of the world," he wrote. "We of Hiroshima invite you to join a worldwide Crusade—of prayer for peace, combining all our prayers with the powerful prayers of Christ's mother in heaven. Is there a motherly heart on earth that does not yearn for peace? How, then, could our Blessed Mother in heaven reject the plea of her children in every country imploring her loving heart to pray and work with us for world peace?"

Father Schiffer's appeal for prayer was powerful, particularly during the age of nuclear escalation and great uncertainty that followed, which still plagues us today.

"The atom bomb has not only brought total destruction, but it may well bring a continuing threat and terror upon mankind, a spiritually dividing effect worse than the physical destruction," he wrote. "We all, living in this atomic age, have the responsibility to do something about it. We all want to promote a real peace."

The Jesuits weren't the only ones convinced that peace is gained by praying the Rosary. In *Ingravescentibus Malis*, an encyclical on the Rosary issued by Pope Pius XI on September 29, 1937, the pope wrote that the Rosary has been used "as a powerful weapon to put the demons to flight, to preserve the integrity of life, to acquire virtue more easily, and in a word to attain real peace among men" (14). And in *Recurrens Mensis*, an apostolic exhortation issued October 7, 1969, Pope Paul VI wrote that "meditating on the mysteries of the Holy Rosary, we will learn the example of Mary, to become peaceful souls, through loving and unceasing contact with Jesus and with the mysteries of his redemptive life."

Our world today is in desperate need of peace. In September 2013, Pope Francis beckoned all people of faith and good will to come together for a worldwide day of fasting and prayer for a peaceful resolution to the ongoing conflicts in Syria, the Middle East, and elsewhere around the globe— during which praying the Rosary was a main portion. While a physical gathering took place at the Vatican, Church leaders around the world encouraged Catholics at home, too, to raise their voices in praying the Rosary for peace. It would be a mistake, though, to conclude that the Rosary should only be prayed to help bring about a peaceful end to major conflicts.

Peace too often eludes us in our own communities, which are experiencing increasing violence and demonstrating an alarming disdain for others who may look, act, or speak differently from what we may consider the "norm." In family life, too, peace is not easy to find. In our communities, large and small, praying the Rosary can be a powerful tool to help maintain harmony, calm heightened emotions, and reorient loved ones back to Christ and one another.

As Pope Pius XI said: "If you desire peace in your hearts, in your homes, and in your country, assemble each evening to recite the Rosary. Let not even one day pass without saying it, no matter how burdened you may be with many cares and labors." For the sake of peace in our world today, we would do well to take his advice.

EXCERPTS FROM *THE ROSARY OF HIROSHIMA*
By Father Hubert F. Schiffer, SJ
Blue Army of Our Lady of Fátima

WORLD PEACE PROMISED FROM HEAVEN

When our Blessed Mother appeared at Fátima, she solemnly declared: "If my requests for prayer and penance are granted, Russia will be converted and there will be peace in the world.

If they are not, Russia will spread its errors throughout the world, provoking wars and persecutions; many good people will be martyred; many nations will be annihilated ... but, finally, my Immaculate Heart will triumph."

The explosion of the first atomic bomb over Hiroshima has initiated a new era. In one frightful second, a proud city of half a million souls was wiped out from the face of the earth. Nothing remained but an "atomic desert," and the word "Hiroshima" became a symbol of total destruction.

To be a survivor of the first atomic bomb in human history, and to have felt its tremendous concussion within the most deadly one-mile radius, gives me the not enviable "advantage" of firsthand experience. Experts have told me that I "ought to be dead." The experts were almost right, for my fellow Jesuits carried me out of the burning city "for a decent Christian funeral."

The atom bomb has not only brought total destruction, but it may well bring a continuing threat and terror upon mankind, a spiritually dividing effect worse than the physical destruction. We all, living in this atomic age, have the responsibility to do something about it. We all want to promote a real peace.

But is there a remedy?

We survivors of Hiroshima bring you a message: the bells of St. Mary's at Hiroshima ring a message of faith, and of hope. Atom-bombed Hiroshima's answer to Our Lady's plea is a crusade of prayer. The fifteen stained-glass windows of the Memorial Shrine will show the mysteries of the Rosary, the prayer which daily unites millions of hearts all over the world.

Do you know anything more moving than a five-year-old laying his little hand into yours and going with you, his eyes shining with confidence in your goodness? We adults have too often forgotten that God is our Creator and Father. We prefer to go our own ways instead of accepting God's guidance. And like them, we run into trouble. We then have to solve "the problem of the atom bomb."

How would you feel as a human father if your children would whisper or chatter together and then look into every corner for a "solution" to their difficulties without ever coming to tell you about them?

We all need and desperately want world peace. And what do we do to attain it? International conferences, economic measures, defense production, civil-defense training. We do almost everything we can think of, except the most important thing: prayer.

Prayer is more powerful than the atom bomb. It promotes and deepens the spirit of human brotherhood.

Americans and Japanese, Germans and French, Chinese and British, Buddhists and Christians—they all need to realize that God is our common Creator and Father. From this realization to the "United Nations" is only one step.

The Shrine for World Peace in the heart of Hiroshima stands as a symbol of this unity. Let us hope that the children who are now playing in its shadow will grow up into a world of peace which we have prepared for them. There in Hiroshima, Americans and Japanese, pilgrims from Australia and Korea, Italy and Canada, are kneeling side by side praying together for peace. This common prayer will reflect itself in common work for peace.

But this is only a beginning. Our atomic age will not be safe as long as prayers are said only at Hiroshima. Not even the prayers there continued day and night will help you if you don't pray, too. What we need today is a Crusade of Prayer, the spirit of prayer everywhere, a renewal of our deepest trust and confidence in God's providence.

Our Blessed Mother promised that when we heeded her plea for prayer and Christian action, the world would have peace. We may feel that our humble efforts cannot have such a tremendous effect upon the world, but let us think for a moment about the power of a river, sweeping everything before it. That river is made up of tiny drops of water, and because numberless tiny drops of rain have fallen into it, the river has become a force that carries heavy ships and changes deserts into fruitful farms and gardens.

So, too, will the Perpetual Rosary Crusade—the recitation of the Rosary for peace by countless persons all over the world—become an immense and irresistible spiritual force for peace. In this universe, there is nothing else that forms a common ground for the peoples of the world except the love of God, charity, and the spirit of prayer. Our Blessed Mother's Rosary is a bond which unites the heart strings of the world.

We of Hiroshima invite you to join a worldwide Crusade— of prayer for peace, combining all our prayers with the powerful prayers of Christ's mother in heaven. Is there a motherly heart on earth that does not yearn for peace? How, then, could our Blessed Mother in heaven reject the plea of her children in every country imploring her loving heart to pray and work with us for world peace?

Bishop Fulton J. Sheen said in one of his radio addresses: "Fátima is not a warning—it is a hope! While man lifts the little atom which he splits to annihilate a world, Mary swings the sun like a trinket on her wrist to convince the world that God has given her the greater power over nature, not for death, but for light and life and hope.... There need not be World War III, and there will not be one if we set the Woman against the Atom."

THE ATOM BOMB

At 2:45 a.m. on August 6, 1945, a B-29 took off from the island of Tinian to drop the first atomic bomb on Japan. Over Iwo Jima it met with an instrument plane and a photography ship. Three weather planes had taken off an hour ahead to scout the sky over three Japanese cities chosen as possible targets: Hiroshima, Nagasaki, and Kokura.

The big flight was on. Soon the first A-bomb would explode only eight city blocks from the Jesuit Church of Our Lady's Assumption where I was stationed in Hiroshima.

The bomb exploded over the city at 8:15 in the morning. It came as a complete surprise, out of a blue and sunny sky. Suddenly, between one breath and another, in the twinkling of an eye, an unearthly, unbearable brightness was all around me; a light unimaginably brilliant, blinding, intense. I could not see, or think. For one short moment, everything was at a standstill. I was left alone swimming in this ocean of light, helpless and frightened. The room seemed to catch its breath in deadly silence.

Suddenly, a terrific explosion filled the air with one bursting thunderstroke. An invisible force lifted me from the chair, hurled me through the air, shook me, battered me, whirled me 'round and 'round like a leaf in a gust of autumn wind.

(Up in the air, the B-29's copilot scribbled in his log: "The flash was terrific. About 25 seconds after the flash we felt two very distinct slaps on the ship. We then turned the ship so that we could observe the results, and there in front of our eyes was without a doubt the greatest explosion man has ever witnessed: the city was nine-tenths covered with smoke of a boiling nature, which seemed to indicate buildings blowing up, and a large column of white cloud which in less than three minutes reached 30,000 and then went to at least 50[,000]-60,000 feet. I am certain the entire crew felt that this experience was more terrifying than any human being had ever thought possible. It seemed impossible to comprehend. Just how many Japanese did we kill? I honestly have the feeling of groping for words to explain this, or I might say, 'My God! What have we done?' If I live a hundred years, I'll never quite get these few minutes out of my mind.")

The light was suddenly gone. All was darkness, silence, nothingness. I was not unconscious, because I was trying to think what was happening. I felt with my fingers in the total blackness enveloping me. I was lying with my face down on broken and splintered pieces of wood, some heavy load pressed on my back, blood was running down my face. I could see nothing, hear no sound. I must be dead, I thought.

Then I heard my own voice. That was the most frightening experience of all, because it showed me I was still alive, and convinced me that some horrible catastrophe had occurred.

An explosion?—Heavens, that was a BOMB! A direct hit!

It took only a second: a flash—fearfully frightening—and Hiroshima, home of half a million people, was wiped off the earth. What was left was only darkness, blood, burns, moans, fire, and spreading terror.

Four Jesuit priests were stationed at the church of Our Lady's Assumption: Father Hugo Lassalle, superior of the whole Jesuit Mission in Japan, and Fathers Kleinsorge, Cieslik, and Schiffer. We spent the whole day in an inferno of flames and smoke before a rescue party was able to reach us. All four were wounded, but through the grace of God we survived.

Nine days later peace came. It was August 15, the feast of our Blessed Mother's assumption.

On the other side of the world, more than a year later, occurred a series of events which on the surface appeared to have no connection, but which have since proved to be the most powerful single force in preventing a repetition of the horrible experience of Hiroshima and Nagasaki.

In Plainfield, New Jersey, a priest had just finished offering a Requiem Mass when he collapsed at the foot of the altar, the victim of an extremely serious heart attack. Doctors gave him only a few weeks to live. But the priest, Rev. Harold V.

Colgan, pastor of St. Mary's Church, Plainfield, completely startled the doctors a few days later when he walked from the hospital a completely cured man, in response to his fervent prayers to the Mother of God.

He promised the Blessed Virgin Mary that if she would obtain from God his complete cure, he would spend the rest of his life spreading devotion to her. He has fulfilled this pledge by starting the Blue Army of Our Lady of Fátima, which has spread to some 25 million persons in 57 nations of the world in observance of the opening quotation in this booklet and the rest of the message given by the Blessed Virgin Mary at Fátima, Portugal, in 1917.

Recognizing that prayer is more powerful than the atom bomb, Father Colgan, who has since been elevated to the rank of Right Reverend Monsignor, thoroughly studied the requests of Our Lady of Fátima and then insisted that each of her requests be fulfilled by the person signing the Blue Army Pledge.

Blue Army members promise to say the Rosary every day, to consecrate themselves to the Blessed Virgin Mary, and show their consecration by wearing the brown scapular, and properly to fulfill the duties of their state in life, offering the sacrifices and penances involved to God in reparation for sin. The Blue Army also urges the first Saturday devotions announced in Fátima.

HISTORY OF FAITH

Since the seventeenth century, Japan had chosen to shut out Christianity from her islands. Before the atom bomb, in

1945, there were hundreds of Buddhist temples and many Buddhist monasteries in Hiroshima. Most of the people had no knowledge of, or interest in, the Christian faith. Many were openly hostile. Our Hiroshima mission counted only two hundred Catholics, about half of whom lived in the villages around the city.

St. Francis Xavier landed in Japan on August 15, 1549, the feast of Our Lady's glorious assumption. Soon hundreds of thousands were baptized, including feudal lords, samurais, and many Buddhist bonzes.

Letters of the first Jesuit missionaries show time and again how these Japanese converts combined deep understanding of Christ's passion with reverence for his Mother, and how they loved to say the Rosary.

Xavier had reason to be proud of his converts: "Among all the nations of the Far East that I know, the Japanese are best disposed towards our Christian way of life."

Three hundred years of cruel persecution could not completely destroy the seeds Xavier had planted. All the early Jesuit and Franciscan missionaries were killed, every known Christian was martyred. But seven generations later, when missionaries were able to return to Japan, they found over 60,000 Catholics hidden in the mountains or in small fishing villages. They still sang the Ave Maria in Latin! They still practiced the daily recitation of the Rosary.

Not only that, they tested the true faith of the new missionary with these three questions: "Are you married? Are you united with the pope in Rome? Do you pay your respects to the Mother of Christ?"

Only then did they tell him: "Father, our hearts are the same as yours. We have kept the faith of our fathers."

CHILDREN PLAY IN THE GARDEN OF THE LIGHT

There can hardly be a doubt but that much abrupt goodwill has been built up by the quiet example of Christian charity during the tragic weeks after the bombing. The Jesuit novitiate in the northern outskirts of Hiroshima became a center for medical first aid and all kinds of assistance. The people will never forget the heroic sacrifices of the Helpers of the Holy Souls. When the whole world seemed to collapse, the Sisters who had lost their convent and all their belongings worked untiringly to help the wounded.

And when kind GIs volunteered to build a small convent for the Sisters, they immediately opened a kindergarten and a day nursery to help the poor mothers in the neighborhood.

In 1947, Japanese Sisters were called to Hiroshima to open an orphanage. There was a crying need for such a home, for thousands of children were wandering around homeless. They slept in holes, under bridges, or in empty freight cars. Unkempt, unwashed, full of lice, and clothed in rags, they looked and acted like alley cats.

Stealing food was the only way to survive, and they banded together to still their continuous hunger. Officials did not know what to do. The few existing institutions were by far not sufficient to take care of so many thousands.

After my recovery from near death under the atom bomb, I was commissioned by Father Lassalle to begin negotiations with state and city officials about the possibilities of opening a house for these children.

All we had at that time was hope; there was no house available, no personnel, no money.

Then came Mother Elizabeth. She was a tiny, smiling, and untiring Japanese nun from Beppu's "Garden of Light" who had promised to help us build a children's home. Mother Elizabeth is a convert. Over a quarter of a century ago she renounced the Shinto religion to become a follower of Christ, whose Sacred Heart is her greatest love. For fifteen years she begged her parents for permission to become a Catholic before they finally heeded her pleas. The daughter of a well-to-do Tokyo family, Mother Elizabeth gave up a life of ease and comfort to bring happiness to Japan's homeless children. Her grandfather was a Shinto priest and her father a doctor.

A brother, Mikihiko Nagata, is author of the bestseller *Father of the Emperor*. A brother-in-law was, for many years, physician to the imperial family, but recently resigned because of his age.

When Australian troops stationed near Hiroshima heard about our plans, they started a "Christmas raffle," and within a few weeks these greathearted men, led by their chaplains, "chipped in" so that the Christ Child had a present of four thousand dollars for his tiny Hiroshima orphans. The Mitsubishi factory offered to sell a large two-story building for the reduced price of $4,000. American GIs meanwhile helped the orphans in their areas with the result that the Japanese more and more admired these kindhearted ambassadors of good will. The Japanese doctors—Buddhists, but with all the universal charity of their profession—donated their time for physical checkups and attendance to sick children. Buddhist temples took up collections of food, and mothers from the neighborhood came with tears in their eyes to offer used clothing.

It was in December of 1947 that the Hiroshima "Garden of Light" began shedding its beams of compassion on homeless children. I will never forget the day when we brought the first group of twelve small children into the old factory. It was a cold afternoon, and we had neither glass nor boards to cover the bombed-out windows.

The children apparently didn't mind these minor details [as] they were used to living and sleeping under the open sky; they played in and around the house and were quite happy. In the evening, we squatted in a large circle on the floor and had our family meal.

Then Mother Elizabeth began to tell a long bedtime story.

Day after day, the Sisters brought more children in. Many of them were sick and had stomach trouble. Soon we had to go begging for more food and blankets. Since food was strictly rationed for everybody, including missionaries and Sisters, and was far not enough, anybody who gave food made a personal sacrifice and had to fast so much the more for it.

And there were other problems. Every drop of water needed in the house had to be carried a distance of several hundred yards. The water carrying became especially trying on cold winter mornings and during the rainy season. It was six months before we had enough money to dig our own well, and the cost was only thirty-five dollars. That amount was akin to a small fortune in the bombed-out city, however.

For many months everyone slept on the floor, because we had no beds. Imagine a house without windows, running water, or food. We had to live from hand to mouth, literally. Our flock of twelve orphans began to grow to fifty. For many pioneering months we didn't need a pantry as there was nothing to put in one. We did not even have a kitchen. The cooking was done in our backyard in the open, with an umbrella over the cook when needed. Army blankets served as overcoats.

It was a hard time, but a happy one. Surrounded with loving care the little ones were forgetting the terror of the long years of war and the horrible aftermath of the dropping of the atom bomb on the city. What we could offer the children was only a roof over their heads, and love. Fortunately, the children liked the "Garden of Light" and called it "home."

The work grew so, and the need was so self-evident that Mayor Hamai offered the Sisters eight thousand square yards of land if they would open another institution in downtown Hiroshima. The Japanese government appropriated seventy-five percent of the necessary funds for building a new structure, practically designed to be extended into a children's hospital in the near future—and soon the new building went up.

Others may term these unfortunate children orphans. Mother Elizabeth will have none of this. These are her children, and she is their mother—in name—and deed—and love. The children share Mother Elizabeth's distaste for the word "orphan." In fact, most of them do not even recognize it as a word that means themselves. Once, some of them saw a motion picture about other war orphans. After the show, they begged Mother to bring the poor unfortunate orphans to their home where they could have a real mother. All this is such joy to the Sisters that they are reluctant to speak of the tremendous amount of hard work. But they are not reluctant to work. Money is still very scarce and every penny must be made to do as much as possible.

Today, nearly 250 children are living, learning, and playing in the new "*Hikari no Sono*" (Garden of Light) in the heart of Hiroshima, and in the children's home at Beppu. The original factory building in Hiroshima's suburb has become a large kindergarten....

A SYMBOL OF WORLD PEACE

The bells of St. Mary's at Hiroshima ring a message of faith, and of hope. They rang out for the first time on Easter Sunday 1953. The four new bells of the Memorial Shrine are a gift of the West German Steel Workers' Union.

Some 20,000 German Catholics took part in the departure festivities before the bells left Germany. Among the speakers on that occasion were the minister-president of North Rhine-Westphalia and the Japanese ambassador to Western Germany. In Hiroshima, the Japanese received these symbolic gifts with special ceremonies. The bells were conducted in a solemn procession from the railroad terminal to the Memorial Shrine. During the procession, a sound truck played a tape recording of the pealing of the bells at the departure ceremony in Germany, and at the same time the arrival of the bells was joyfully announced over the Hiroshima radio station.

Recently, the City Council of Cologne has presented Hiroshima with a pipe organ to be installed in the new shrine of our Blessed Mother. With the organ goes a plaque reading: "Cologne and Hiroshima, bound through common suffering, work and pray for world peace." The city of Bonn, capital of the Federal German Republic, has donated the tabernacle for the Memorial Shrine. The walls and the doors of the tabernacle depict the Fall of Man, the Deluge and the ruins of Hiroshima. Above them, pointing upward, is the protective hand of the Redeemer and the inscription: "*Pax Christi.*"

Atom-bombed Hiroshima's answer to Our Lady's pleas at Fátima is a crusade of prayer. Fifteen stained-glass windows show the mysteries of the Rosary, the prayer which daily unites millions of hearts all over the world. The shrine is a symbol of this unity.

But this is only a beginning. The prayers said at Hiroshima, continued day and night, can avail only if you pray, too.

Our Japanese friends unite their prayers with ours. They love to recite with us the century-old prayer to Mary, the Queen of Peace:

"Remember, O most gracious Virgin Mary, that never was it known that anyone who fled to thy protection, implored thy help or sought thy intercession was left unaided. Inspired with this confidence, I fly to thee, O Virgin of Virgins, my Mother. To thee I come, before thee I stand, sinful and sorrowful. O Mother of the Word Incarnate, despise not my petition, but in thy mercy, hear and answer me."

This spirit of prayer can and will bring peace. Father Peyton has said so well: "The family that prays together, stays together." Isn't that true also in the family of nations?

This is the message of Hiroshima: Prayer in every heart, prayer on every lip, prayer moving the work of every hand throughout the world. It is this spirit of prayer that will bring us peace in this world.

Will this come true? — The answer is up to you....

WHAT YOU CAN DO

Regardless of where you live in the world, you can participate in the Crusade for World Peace through your prayers and sacrifices. Make up your mind now that you will recite the Rosary every day, that you will consecrate yourself to the Immaculate Heart of Mary and wear her brown scapular; that you will offer to heaven in reparation of sin, the sacrifices and penances involved in the proper fulfillment of the duties of your state in life.

CHAPTER SIX

To Fight Evil

In April 2014, an attack occurred that, for a short time at least, seemed to unite the world. The Nigeria-based terrorist organization Boko Haram kidnapped 276 young girls, leaving the world stunned and demanding their return via news outlets and social media. It was too late, however. They had disappeared. The battle against terrorism is one Nigeria has been fighting, with mixed success, for years.

In an interview in March 2016, Bishop Oliver Dashe Doeme of the Diocese of Maiduguri said that since being named a bishop in 2009 more than 40 percent of the Catholic population had disappeared from his diocese. "Even the priests had to run for their lives," he said. "They couldn't have stayed, and even if they did stay, who would they minister to? Even the female religious had to run for their dear lives, and their convents [were] destroyed. It has been really devastating to our people."

But because of a remarkable vision, Bishop Doeme is convinced that the key to defeating Boko Haram rests firmly in our Blessed Mother and, of course, the Rosary. Toward the end of 2014, when the threat from Boko Haram was particularly strong, Bishop Doeme said he received a vision of Jesus while praying the Rosary in his chapel in the presence of the Blessed Sacrament. Jesus didn't say a word, but rather handed Bishop Doeme a sword. When he reached out to take it, the sword turned into a Rosary. Then Jesus spoke, saying three times, "Boko Haram is gone."

"I didn't need any prophet to give me the explanation," Bishop Doeme told Catholic News Agency. "It was clear that with the Rosary we would be able to expel Boko Haram." He has since worked to spread devotion to the Rosary and has asked his people—and all people—to use it to pray for an end to evil.

Bishop Doeme's story is perhaps the most recent in a long line of testimonials crediting the Rosary for protection against evil. In the Battle of Lepanto, which occurred in 1571, and from which the feast of Our Lady of Victory (later renamed the feast of Our Lady of the Rosary) found its source, the Rosary was credited with defeating the Ottoman Empire and thereby saving Christianity in Western Europe.

Padre Pio referred to the Rosary as "my weapon" and, according to sources, wore it around his arm every night.

In the text that follows, written in September 1951, Pope Pius XII put forth the Rosary as an antidote to the evils facing the world at the time. Fewer than ten years after the end of World War II, the Korean War was underway. The nuclear age was in full gear. Communism was on the rise. There was plenty of reason to be wary of what he called "the calamitous conditions of our times."

In the early twenty-first century, we too find ourselves facing calamitous times. War is raging in the Middle East, while terrorism is increasingly present at home and abroad. The persecution of Christians is happening—blatantly in some cases, more subtly in others. It feels like there is much to fear. But Mary did not want us to fear; she wanted us to pray. According to the promises made to St. Dominic, Mary promised special graces and protection to those who prayed the Rosary, and called the Rosary a "very powerful armor against hell" that "will destroy vice, deliver from sin, and dispel heresy."

A powerful example of this is Blessed Bartolo Longo, an Italian born in 1841. Longo had dabbled in the occult—even declaring himself a satanic priest—before undergoing a conversion to Catholicism. The Rosary was a large part of that conversion, and he was encouraged to pray it constantly by his spiritual director. But it wasn't until he received a message one day while walking through a field, filled with anxiety, that his conversion was complete. In *History of the Sanctuary of Pompei, dedicated to the Most Blessed Virgin of the Rosary*, he wrote about this event:

> All Nature lay wrapt [sic] in the deepest silence. I looked around me; not even the shadow of a living soul. Suddenly I came to a dead stop; my heart was bursting within me. In such darkness of being it seemed to me as though a friendly voice were whispering to me those same words that I had read, and that a true and holy friend of mine, now gone to his rest, was wont to repeat to me: "If you seek to be saved promulgate the Rosary. This is dear Mary's own promise." Who promulgates the Rosary is safe! This thought was like the lightning that flashes through

the clouds on a dark and stormy night. Satan, who had held me as his prey, saw his defeat drawing near, and in a last desperate effort wound his coils more closely around me. It was the last battle, but a most terrible one. With the audacity born of despair I raised my brow and my hands toward Heaven, and addressing myself to the sweet Mother-Maid: "If it is true"—I cried out, "that Thou didst promise to Saint Domenic that whosoever should promulgate Thy Rosary should be saved, then I will be saved, for I shall not leave this valley without having propagated Thy Rosary." No voice answered me; silence as of the grave encompassed me around. But suddenly a great calm succeeded to the dreadful tempest in my soul, and I felt that perhaps someday my cry of anguish would be answered.... And so I resolutely determined with all my powers to promote the devotion to the Rosary in this desolate valley, where by a strange disposition of Providence I found myself, at the time.

Longo was true to his word, spending the rest of his life promulgating the Rosary until his death in 1926 at age 85. On his deathbed, he credited the Blessed Mother for his salvation from evil. "My only desire is to see Mary who saved me," he said, "and who will save me from the clutches of Satan." Longo's story is just as relevant now, as it was then, as we face a world of evils today. If we pray the Rosary, we too shall be saved!

INGRUENTIUM MALORUM
Encyclical on reciting the Rosary
by Pope Pius XII

To our Venerable Brethren, patriarchs, primates, archbishops, bishops, and other ordinaries having peace and communion with the Apostolic See

Venerable Brethren,
Greetings and Apostolic Benediction.

Ever since we were raised, by the design of Divine Providence, to the supreme Chair of Peter, we have never ceased, in the face of approaching evils, to entrust to the most powerful protection of the Mother of God the destiny of the human family, and, to this end, as you know, we have from time to time written letters of exhortation.

2. You know, Venerable Brethren, with what zeal and with what spontaneous and unanimous approval the Christian people everywhere have answered our invitation. It has been magnificently testified many times by the great demonstration of faith and love towards the august Queen of Heaven, and above all, by that manifestation of universal joy which, last year, our eyes had the pleasure to behold, when, in St. Peter's Square, surrounded by an immense multitude of the faithful, we solemnly proclaimed the assumption into heaven of the Virgin Mary, body and soul.

3. The recollection of these things comes back pleasantly to us and encourages us to trust firmly in Divine Mercy. How-

ever, at present, we do not lack reasons for profound sorrow which torment and sadden our paternal heart.

4. You know well, Venerable Brethren, the calamitous conditions of our times. Fraternal harmony among nations, shattered for so long a time, has not yet been reestablished everywhere. On the contrary, here and there, we see souls upset by hatred and rivalry, while threats of new bloody conflicts still hover over the peoples. To this, one must add the violent storm of persecution, which in many parts of the world has been unleashed against the Church, depriving it of its liberty, saddening it very cruelly with calumnies and miseries of all kinds, and making the blood of martyrs flow again and again.

5. To what and to how many snares are the souls of so many of our sons submitted in those areas to make them reject the faith of their fathers, and to make them break, most wretchedly, the bond of union which links them to this Apostolic See! Nor can we pass over in silence a new crime to which, with utmost sorrow, we want earnestly to draw not only your attention, but the attention of the clergy, of parents, and even of public authorities. We refer to the iniquitous campaign that the impious lead everywhere to harm the shining souls of children. Not even the age of innocence has been spared, for, alas, there are not lacking those who boldly dare to snatch from the mystical garden of the Church even the most beautiful flowers, which constitute the hope of religion and society. Considering this, one cannot be surprised if peoples groan under the weight of the Divine punishment, and live under the fear of even greater calamities.

6. However, consideration of a situation so pregnant with dangers must not depress your souls, Venerable Brethren. Instead, mindful of that Divine teaching: "Ask and it shall be given to you; seek and you shall find; knock, and it shall be opened to you" (Lk 11:9), fly with greater confidence to the Mother of God. There, the Christian people have always sought chief refuge in the hour of danger, because "she has been constituted the cause of salvation for the whole human race" (St. Irenaeus).

7. Therefore, we look forward with joyful expectation and revived hope to the coming month of October, during which the faithful are accustomed to flock in larger numbers to the churches to raise their supplications to Mary by means of the Holy Rosary.

8. O Venerable Brethren, we desire that, this year, this prayer should be offered with such greater fervor of heart as is demanded by the increased urgency of the need. We well know the Rosary's powerful efficacy to obtain the maternal aid of the Virgin. By no means is there only one way to pray to obtain this aid. However, we consider the Holy Rosary the most convenient and most fruitful means, as is clearly suggested by the very origin of this practice, heavenly rather than human, and by its nature. What prayers are better adapted and more beautiful than the Lord's Prayer and the angelic salutation, which are the flowers with which this mystical crown is formed? With meditation of the Sacred Mysteries added to the vocal prayers, there emerges another very great advantage, so that all, even the most simple and least educated, have in this a prompt and easy way to nourish and preserve their own faith.

9. And truly, from the frequent meditation on the Mysteries, the soul little by little and imperceptibly draws and absorbs the virtues they contain, and is wondrously enkindled with a longing for things immortal, and becomes strongly and easily impelled to follow the path which Christ himself and his Mother have followed. The recitation of identical formulas repeated so many times, rather than rendering the prayer sterile and boring, has on the contrary the admirable quality of infusing confidence in him who prays and brings to bear a gentle compulsion on the motherly Heart of Mary.

10. Let it be your particular care, O Venerable Brethren, that the faithful, on the occasion of the coming month of October, should use this most fruitful form of prayer with the utmost possible zeal, and that it become always more esteemed and more diligently recited.

11. Through your efforts, the Christian people should be led to understand the dignity, the power, and the excellence of the Rosary.

12. But it is above all in the bosom of the family that we desire the custom of the Holy Rosary to be everywhere adopted, religiously preserved, and ever more intensely practiced. In vain is a remedy sought for the wavering fate of civil life, if the family, the principle and foundation of the human community, is not fashioned after the pattern of the Gospel.

13. To undertake such a difficult duty, we affirm that the custom of the family recitation of the Holy Rosary is a most efficacious means. What a sweet sight—most pleasing to God—when, at eventide, the Christian home resounds with the frequent repetition of praises in honor of the august Queen

of Heaven! Then the Rosary, recited in common, assembles before the image of the Virgin, in an admirable union of hearts, the parents and their children, who come back from their daily work. It unites them piously with those absent and those dead. It links all more tightly in a sweet bond of love, with the most Holy Virgin, who, like a loving mother, in the circle of her children, will be there bestowing upon them an abundance of the gifts of concord and family peace.

14. Then the home of the Christian family, like that of Nazareth, will become an earthly abode of sanctity, and, so to speak, a sacred temple, where the Holy Rosary will not only be the particular prayer which every day rises to heaven in an odor of sweetness, but will also form the most efficacious school of Christian discipline and Christian virtue. This meditation on the Divine Mysteries of the Redemption will teach the adults to live, admiring daily the shining examples of Jesus and Mary, and to draw from these examples comfort in adversity, striving towards those heavenly treasures "where neither thief draws near, nor moth destroys" (Lk 12:33). This meditation will bring to the knowledge of the little ones the main truths of the Christian faith, making love for the Redeemer blossom almost spontaneously in their innocent hearts; while seeing their parents kneeling before the majesty of God, they will learn from their very early years how great before the throne of God is the value of prayers said in common.

15. We do not hesitate to affirm again publicly that we put great confidence in the Holy Rosary for the healing of evils which afflict our times. Not with force, not with arms, not with human power, but with Divine help obtained through

the means of this prayer, strong like David with his sling, the Church undaunted shall be able to confront the infernal enemy, repeating to him the words of the young shepherd: "Thou comest to me with a sword, and a spear, and with a shield; but I come to thee in the name of the Lord of Hosts, the God of armies ... and all this assembly shall know that the Lord saveth not with sword and spear, for this is his battle, and he will deliver you into our hands" (1 Kgs 17:45-47).

16. For this reason, we earnestly desire, Venerable Brethren, that all the faithful, following your example and your exhortation, should respond solicitously to our paternal exhortation, uniting their hearts and their voices with the same ardor of charity. If the evils and the assaults of the wicked increase, so likewise must the piety of all good people increase and become ever more vigorous. Let them strive to obtain from our most loving Mother, especially through this form of prayer, that better times may quickly return for the Church and society.

17. May the very powerful Mother of God, moved by the prayers of so many of her sons, obtain from her only Son— let us all beseech her—that those who have miserably wandered from the path of truth and virtue may, with new fervor, find it again; that hatred and rivalry, which are the sources of discord and every kind of mishap, may be put aside, and that a true, just, and genuine peace may shine again upon individuals, families, peoples, and nations. And, finally, may she obtain that, after the rights of the Church have been secured in accord with justice, its beneficent influence may penetrate without obstacle the hearts of men, the social classes, and the avenues of public life so as to join people among themselves

in brotherhood and lead them to that prosperity which regulates, preserves, and coordinates the rights and duties of all without harming anyone and which daily makes for greater and greater mutual friendship and collaboration.

18. Venerable Brethren and beloved sons, while you entwine new flowers of supplication by reciting your Rosary, do not forget those who languish miserably in prison camps, jails, and concentration camps. There are among them, as you know, also bishops dismissed from their sees solely for having heroically defended the sacred rights of God and the Church. There are sons, fathers, and mothers, wrested from their homes and compelled to lead unhappy lives far away in unknown lands and strange climates.

19. Just as we love them with a special charity and embrace them with the love of a father, so must you, with a brotherly love which the Christian religion nourishes and enkindles, join with us before the altar of the Virgin Mother of God and recommend them to her motherly heart. She doubtlessly will, with exquisite sweetness, revive in their hearts the hope of eternal reward and, we firmly believe, will not fail to hasten the end of so much sorrow.

20. We do not doubt that you, O Venerable Brethren, with your usual burning zeal, will bring to the knowledge of your clergy and people these our paternal exhortations in a way which will appear most appropriate to you.

21. Feeling certain that our sons throughout the world will respond willingly and generously to this our invitation, we impart, from the fullness of our heart and as an evidence of our favor and an augury of heavenly graces, to each and

every one of you, to the flock entrusted to each of you and particularly to those who, especially during the month of October, will devoutly recite the Holy Rosary according to our intentions, our Apostolic Blessing.

Given in Rome, at St. Peter's, the 15th day of September, the feast of the Seven Sorrows of the Virgin Mary, in the year 1951, the thirteenth of our pontificate.

CHAPTER SEVEN

To Combat Secularism

Thirteen. That's an important number in a recent study, conducted by the Center for Applied Research in the Apostolate at Georgetown University (CARA), on why young people are leaving the Faith. According to CARA's research, thirteen was the typical age in which young people made the decision that Catholicism wasn't for them. And when asked if they were ever likely to return to the Faith after they had left it, only 13 percent of those surveyed responded in the affirmative. Both statistics are disturbing, to say the least.

Looking more deeply at the study, the main reason young people gave for leaving the Faith was that they no longer believed in God or religion. The same reasoning—a lack of belief—held true for adults when surveyed by the Pew Research Center in 2015. For both young people and adults, their religious beliefs didn't hold up when compared to other things, including what they identified as science, logic, evidence, and common sense.

This growing disbelief is just one of the results of increasing secularism in the West and particularly the United States. This secularism today is manifested in the increasing lack of tolerance of religious practice by governments and the increasing lack of participation of members of society in organized religion. In an address to the U.S. bishops during their *ad limina* visit to Rome in January 2012, Pope Benedict XVI spoke of the pervasiveness of secularism in American society, saying, "It is imperative that the entire Catholic community in the United States come to realize the grave threats to the Church's public moral witness presented by a radical secularism which finds increasing expression in the political and cultural spheres."

He continued: "The seriousness of these threats needs to be clearly appreciated at every level of ecclesial life. Of particular concern are certain attempts being made to limit that most cherished of American freedoms, the freedom of religion. Many of you have pointed out that concerted efforts have been made to deny the right of conscientious objection on the part of Catholic individuals and institutions with regard to cooperation in intrinsically evil practices. Others have spoken to me of a worrying tendency to reduce religious freedom to mere freedom of worship without guarantees of respect for freedom of conscience. Here once more we see the need for an engaged, articulate, and well-formed Catholic laity endowed with a strong critical sense vis-à-vis the dominant culture and with the courage to counter a reductive secularism which would delegitimize the Church's participation in public debate about the issues which are determining the future of American society. The preparation of committed lay leaders and the presentation of a convincing articulation of the Christian vision of man and society remain a primary task of the Church in your country; as essential components of the New Evangelization, these concerns must shape the vision and goals of catechetical programs at every level."

The roots of secularism run deep, and Pope Benedict wasn't the first or only pontiff to warn against it. The pontificate of Pope Leo XIII, who reigned from 1878 to 1903, was plagued by politics and the drama of atheist humanism. In several portions of his astounding eleven encyclicals on the Rosary, one of which follows below, Pope Leo spoke about the dangers of a world without belief. He spoke from experience. The nineteenth century proved to be fertile ground for a number of notable figures, including Friedrich Nietzsche, Karl Marx, and Ludwig Feuerbach, who attempted to construct an understanding of the person apart from God. Such thought claimed that a person's worth existed only in what they were able to produce, and this period paved the way for the contemporary atheism of today that claims to have advanced beyond God.

With the rise of atheist and secular humanists, Pope Leo worked to prevent the common man from being swayed by their arguments. He responded by holding up the Church's devotional life as the key to everyday holiness—the tools to overcome the temptations of the godless. One of the key tools of this prayer was the Rosary, for which he had a deep affection. Known as "the pope of the Rosary," Pope Leo XIII wrote his encyclicals on the Marian devotion's many benefits in fighting the difficulties of the day, including secularism. In *Supremi Apostolatus Officio*, he wrote: "The Rosary is the most excellent form of prayer and the most efficacious means of attaining eternal life. It is the remedy for all our evils, the root of all our blessings. There is no more excellent way of praying."

Pope Leo was right. In a world in which the drum of secularism beats loudly and enticingly, the quiet prayer of the Rosary is a sure and steadfast way to keep our lives and hearts focused on what matters: Jesus Christ. Then, perhaps, will we be able to slowly shift from a culture with a growing lack of belief to one with an abundance of belief—and one in which the number thirteen doesn't mean the ominous things it means today.

Octobri Mense
Encyclical on the Rosary
by Pope Leo XIII

To our Venerable Brethren the patriarchs, primates, archbishops, bishops, and other ordinaries having grace and communion with the Apostolic See.

Venerable Brethren,
Greeting and Apostolic Benediction.

At the coming of the month of October, dedicated and consecrated as it is to the Blessed Virgin of the Rosary, we recall with satisfaction the instant exhortations which in preceding years we addressed to you, Venerable Brethren, desiring, as we did, that the faithful, urged by your authority and by your zeal, should redouble their piety towards the august Mother of God, the mighty helper of Christians, and should pray to her throughout the month, invoking her by that most holy rite of the Rosary which the Church, especially in the passage of difficult times, has ever used for the accomplishment of all desires. This year once again do we publish our wishes, once again do we encourage you by the same exhortations. We are persuaded to this in love for the Church, whose sufferings, far from mitigating, increase daily in number and in gravity. Universal and well-known are the evils we deplore: war made upon the sacred dogmas which the Church holds and transmits; derision cast upon the integrity of that Christian morality which she has in keeping; enmity declared, with the impudence of audacity and with criminal malice, against the very Christ, as though the Divine work of Redemption itself were to be destroyed from its foundation— that work which, indeed, no adverse power shall ever utterly abolish or destroy.

2. No new events are these in the career of the Church militant. Jesus foretold them to his disciples. That she may teach men the truth and may guide them to eternal salvation, she must enter upon a daily war; and throughout the course of ages she has fought, even to martyrdom, rejoicing and glorifying herself in nothing more than in the occasion of signing her cause with her Founder's blood, the sure and certain pledge of the victory whereof she holds the promise. Nevertheless, we must not conceal the profound sadness with which this necessity of constant war afflicts the righteous. It is indeed a cause of great sorrow that so many should be deterred and led astray by error and enmity to God; that so many should be indifferent to all forms of religion, and should finally become estranged from faith; that so many Catholics should be such in name only, and should pay to religion no honor or worship. And still sadder and more beset with anxieties grows the soul at the thought of the fruitful source of most manifold evils existing in the organization of states that allow no place to the Church, and that oppose her

championship of holy virtue. This is truly a terrible manifestation of the just vengeance of God, who allows blindness of soul to darken upon the nations that forsake him. These are evils that cry aloud, that cry of themselves with a daily increasing voice. It is absolutely necessary that the Catholic voice should also call to God with unwearied instance, "without ceasing" (1 Thes 5:17); that the faithful should pray not only in their own homes, but in public, gathered together under the sacred roof; that they should beseech urgently the all-foreseeing God to deliver the Church from evil men (2 Thes 3:2) and to bring back the troubled nations to good sense and reason, by the light and love of Christ.

3. Wonderful and beyond hope or belief is this. The world goes on its laborious way, proud of its riches, of its power, of its arms, of its genius; the Church goes onward along the course of ages with an even step, trusting in God only, to whom, day and night, she lifts her eyes and her suppliant hands. Even though in her prudence she neglects not the human aid which Providence and the times afford her, not in these does she put her trust, which rests in prayer, in supplication, in the invocation of God. Thus it is that she renews her vital breath; the diligence of her prayer has caused her, in her aloofness from worldly things and in her continual union with the Divine will, to live the tranquil and peaceful life of our very Lord Jesus Christ; being herself the image of Christ, whose happy and perpetual joy was hardly marred by the horror of the torments he endured for us. This important doctrine of Christian wisdom has been ever believed and practiced by Christians worthy of the name. Their prayers rise to God eagerly and more frequently when the cunning

and the violence of the perverse afflict the Church and her supreme Pastor. Of this the faithful of the Church in the East gave an example that should be offered to the imitation of posterity. Peter, Vicar of Jesus Christ, and first pontiff of the Church, had been cast into prison, loaded with chains by the guilty Herod, and left for certain death. None could carry him, help or snatch him from the peril. But there was the certain help that fervent prayer wins from God. The Church, as the sacred story tells us, made prayer without ceasing to God for him (Acts 12:5); and the greater was the fear of a misfortune, the greater was the fervor of all who prayed to God. After the granting of their desires the miracle stood revealed; and Christians still celebrate with a joyous gratitude the marvel of the deliverance of Peter. Christ has given us a still more memorable instance, a Divine instance, so that the Church might be formed not upon his precepts only, but upon his example also. During his whole life he had given himself to frequent and fervent prayer, and in the supreme hours in the Garden of Gethsemane, when his soul was filled with bitterness and sorrow unto death, he prayed to his Father and prayed repeatedly (Lk 22:44). It was not for himself that he prayed thus, for he feared nothing and needed nothing, being God; he prayed for us, for his Church, whose prayers and future tears he already then accepted with joy, to give them back in mercies.

4. But since the salvation of our race was accomplished by the mystery of the Cross, and since the Church, dispenser of that salvation after the triumph of Christ, was founded upon earth and instituted, Providence established a new order for a new people. The consideration of the divine coun-

sels is united to the great sentiment of religion. The eternal Son of God, about to take upon him our nature for the saving and ennobling of man, and about to consummate thus a mystical union between himself and all mankind, did not accomplish his design without adding there the free consent of the elect Mother, who represented in some sort all human kind, according to the illustrious and just opinion of St. Thomas, who says that the Annunciation was effected with the consent of the Virgin standing in the place of humanity. With equal truth may it be also affirmed that, by the will of God, Mary is the intermediary through whom is distributed unto us this immense treasure of mercies gathered by God, for mercy and truth were created by Jesus Christ (Jn 1:17). Thus as no man goeth to the Father but by the Son, so no man goeth to Christ but by his Mother. How great are the goodness and mercy revealed in this design of God! What a correspondence with the frailty of man! We believe in the infinite goodness of the Most High, and we rejoice in it; we believe also in his justice, and we fear it. We adore the beloved Savior, lavish of his blood and of his life; we dread the inexorable Judge. Thus do those whose actions have disturbed their consciences need an intercessor mighty in favor with God, merciful enough not to reject the cause of the desperate, merciful enough to lift up again towards hope in the divine mercy the afflicted and the broken down. Mary is this glorious intermediary; she is the mighty Mother of the Almighty; but—what is still sweeter—she is gentle, extreme in tenderness, of a limitless loving-kindness. As such God gave her to us. Having chosen her for the Mother of his only begotten Son, he taught her all a mother's feeling that breathes nothing but pardon and love. Such Christ desired she should be, for he consented to be subject to Mary and to obey her as a son a mother. Such he proclaimed her from the cross, when he entrusted to her care and love the whole of the race of man in the person of his disciple John. Such, finally, she proves herself by her courage in gathering in the heritage of the enormous labors of her Son, and in accepting the charge of her maternal duties towards us all.

5. The design of this most dear mercy, realized by God in Mary and confirmed by the testament of Christ, was comprehended at the beginning, and accepted with the utmost joy by the holy apostles and the earliest believers. It was the counsel and teaching of the venerable Fathers of the Church. All the nations of the Christian age received it with one mind; and even when literature and tradition are silent there is a voice that breaks from every Christian breast and speaks with all eloquence. No other reason is needed than that of a divine faith which, by a powerful and most pleasant impulse, persuades us towards Mary. Nothing is more natural, nothing more desirable than to seek a refuge in the protection and in the loyalty of her to whom we may confess our designs and our actions, our innocence and our repentance, our torments and our joys, our prayers and our desires—all our affairs. All men, moreover, are filled with the hope and confidence that petitions which might be received with less favor from the lips of unworthy men, God will accept when they are recommended by the most holy Mother, and will grant with all favors. The truth and the sweetness of these thoughts bring to the soul an unspeakable comfort; but they inspire all the more compassion for those who, being without divine faith, honor not Mary and have her not for their mother; for those also who, holding Christian faith,

dare to accuse of excess the devotion to Mary, thereby sorely wounding filial piety.

6. This storm of evils, in the midst of which the Church struggles so strenuously, reveals to all her pious children the holy duty whereto they are bound to pray to God with instance, and the manner in which they may give to their prayers the greater power. Faithful to the religious example of our fathers, let us have recourse to Mary, our holy Sovereign. Let us entreat, let us beseech, with one heart, Mary, the Mother of Jesus Christ, our Mother. "Show thyself to be a mother; cause our prayers to be accepted by him who, born for us, consented to be thy Son."

7. Now, among the several rites and manners of paying honor to the Blessed Mary, some are to be preferred, inasmuch as we know them to be most powerful and most pleasing to our Mother; and for this reason we specially mention by name and recommend the Rosary. The common language has given the name of corona to this manner of prayer, which recalls to our minds the great mysteries of Jesus and Mary united in joys, sorrows, and triumphs. The contemplation of these august mysteries, contemplated in their order, affords to faithful souls a wonderful confirmation of faith, protection against the disease of error, and increase of the strength of the soul. The soul and memory of him who thus prays, enlightened by faith, are drawn towards these mysteries by the sweetest devotion, are absorbed therein and are surprised before the work of the Redemption of mankind, achieved at such a price and by events so great. The soul is filled with gratitude and love before these proofs of divine love; its hope becomes enlarged and its desire is increased

for those things which Christ has prepared for such as have united themselves to him in imitation of his example and in participation in his sufferings. The prayer is composed of words proceeding from God himself, from the Archangel Gabriel, and from the Church; full of praise and of high desires; and it is renewed and continued in an order at once fixed and various; its fruits are ever new and sweet.

8. Moreover, we may well believe that the Queen of Heaven herself has granted an especial efficacy to this mode of supplication, for it was by her command and counsel that the devotion was begun and spread abroad by the holy patriarch Dominic as a most potent weapon against the enemies of the Faith at an epoch not, indeed, unlike our own, of great danger to our holy religion. The heresy of the Albigenses had in effect, one while covertly, another while openly, overrun many countries, and this most vile offspring of the Manicheans, whose deadly errors it reproduced, were the cause in stirring up against the Church the most bitter animosity and a virulent persecution. There seemed to be no human hope of opposing this fanatical and most pernicious sect when timely succor came from on high through the instrument of Mary's Rosary. Thus under the favor of the powerful Virgin, the glorious vanquisher of all heresies, the forces of the wicked were destroyed and dispersed, and faith issued forth unharmed and more shining than before. All manner of similar instances are widely recorded, and both ancient and modern history furnish remarkable proofs of nations saved from perils and winning benedictions therefrom. There is another signal argument in favor of this devotion, inasmuch as from the very moment of its institution it was immedi-

ately encouraged and put into most frequent practice by all classes of society. In truth, the piety of the Christian people honors, by many titles and in multiform ways, the divine Mother, who, alone most admirable among all creatures, shines resplendent in unspeakable glory. But this title of the Rosary, this mode of prayer which seems to contain, as it were, a final pledge of affection, and to sum up in itself the honor due to Our Lady, has always been highly cherished and widely used in private and in public, in homes and in families, in the meetings of confraternities, at the dedication of shrines, and in solemn processions; for there has seemed to be no better means of conducting sacred solemnities, or of obtaining protection and favors.

9. Nor may we permit to pass unnoticed the especial providence of God displayed in this devotion; for through the lapse of time religious fervor has sometimes seemed to diminish in certain nations, and even this pious method of prayer has fallen into disuse; but piety and devotion have again flourished and become vigorous in a most marvelous manner, when, either through the grave situation of the commonwealth or through some pressing public necessity, general recourse has been had—more to this than to even other means of obtaining help—to the Rosary, whereby it has been restored to its place of honor on the altars. But there is no need to seek for examples of this power in a past age, since we have in the present a signal instance of it. In these times—so troublous (as we have said before) for the Church, and so heart-rending for ourselves—set as we are by the Divine Will at the helm, it is still given us to note with admiration the great zeal and fervor with which Mary's

Rosary is honored and recited in every place and nation of the Catholic world. And this circumstance, which assuredly is to be attributed to the divine action and direction upon men, rather than to the wisdom and efforts of individuals, strengthens and consoles our heart, filling us with great hope for the ultimate and most glorious triumph of the Church under the auspices of Mary.

10. But there are some who, whilst they honestly agree with what we have said, yet because their hopes—especially as regard the peace and tranquillity of the Church—have not yet been fulfilled, nay, rather because troubles seem to augment, have ceased to pray with diligence and fervor, in a fit of discouragement. Let these look into themselves and labor that the prayers they address to God may be made in a proper spirit, according to the precept of our Lord Jesus Christ. And if there be such, let them reflect how unworthy and how wrong it is to wish to assign to almighty God the time and the manner of giving his assistance, since he owes nothing to us, and when he hearkens to our supplications and crowns our merits, he only crowns his own innumerable benefits [according to St. Augustine]; and when he complies least with our wishes it is as a good father towards his children, having pity on their childishness and consulting their advantage. But as regards the prayers which we join to the suffrages of the heavenly citizens, and offer humbly to God to obtain his mercy for the Church, they are always favorably received and heard, and either obtain for the Church great and imperishable benefits, or their influence is temporarily withheld for a time of greater need. In truth, to these supplications is added an immense weight and grace—the

prayers and merits of Christ our Lord, who has loved the Church and has delivered himself up for her to sanctify her … so that he should be glorified in her (Eph 5:25-27). He is her Sovereign Head, holy, innocent, always living to make intercession for us, on whose prayers and supplication we can always by divine authority rely. As for what concerns the exterior and temporal prosperity of the Church, it is evident that she has to cope with most malicious and powerful adversaries. Too often has she suffered at their hands the abolition of her rights, the diminution and oppression of her liberties, scorn and affronts to her authority, and every conceivable outrage. And if in their wickedness her enemies have not accomplished all the injury they had resolved upon and striven to do, they nevertheless seem to go on unchecked. But, despite them the Church, amidst all these conflicts, will always stand out and increase in greatness and glory. Nor can human reason rightly understand why evil, apparently so dominant, should yet be so restricted as regards its results; whilst the Church, driven into straits, comes forth glorious and triumphant. And she ever remains more steadfast in virtue because she draws men to the acquisition of the ultimate good. And since this is her mission, her prayers must have much power to effect the end and purpose of God's providential and merciful designs towards men. Thus, when men pray with and through the Church, they at length obtain what almighty God has designed from all eternity to bestow upon mankind (*Summa Theologica*). The subtlety of the human intelligence fails now to grasp the high designs of Providence; but the time will come when, through the goodness of God, causes and effects will be made clear, and the marvelous power and utility of prayer will be shown forth. Then it will be seen how many in the midst of a corrupt age have kept themselves pure and inviolate from all concupiscence of the flesh and the spirit, working out their sanctification in the fear of God (2 Cor 7:1); how others, when exposed to the danger of temptation, have without delay restrained themselves gaining new strength for virtue from the peril itself; how others, having fallen, have been seized with the ardent desire to be restored to the embraces of a compassionate God. Therefore, with these reflections before them, we beseech all again and again not to yield to the deceits of the old enemy, nor for any cause whatsoever to cease from the duty of prayer. Let their prayers be persevering, let them pray without intermission; let their first care be to supplicate for the sovereign good—the eternal salvation of the whole world, and the safety of the Church. Then they may ask from God other benefits for the use and comfort of life, returning thanks always, whether their desires are granted or refused, as to a most indulgent father. Finally, may they converse with God with the greatest piety and devotion according to the example of the saints, and that of our Most Holy Master and Redeemer, with great cries and tears (Heb 5:7).

11. Our fatherly solicitude urges us to implore of God, the giver of all good gifts, not merely the spirit of prayer, but also that of holy penance for all the sons of the Church. And whilst we make this most earnest supplication, we exhort all and each one to the practice with equal fervor of both these virtues combined. Thus prayer fortifies the soul, makes it strong for noble endeavors, leads it up to divine things: penance enables us to overcome ourselves, especially our bodies—most inveterate enemies of reason and the evangelical

law. And it is very clear that these virtues unite well with each other, assist each other mutually, and have the same object, namely, to detach man born for heaven from perishable objects, and to raise him up to heavenly commerce with God. On the other hand, the mind that is excited by passions and enervated by pleasure is insensible to the delights of heavenly things, and makes cold and neglectful prayers quite unworthy of being accepted by God. We have before our eyes examples of the penance of holy men whose prayers and supplications were consequently most pleasing to God, and even obtained miracles. They governed and kept assiduously in subjection their minds and hearts and wills. They accepted with the greatest joy and humility the doctrines of Christ and the teachings of his Church. Their unique desire was to advance in the science of God; nor had their actions any other object than the increase of his glory. They restrained most severely their passions, treated their bodies rudely and harshly, abstaining from even permitted pleasures through love of virtue. And, therefore, most deservedly could they have said with the apostle Paul, our conversation is in heaven (Phil 3:20): hence the potent efficacy of their prayers in appeasing and in supplicating the Divine Majesty. It is clear that not everyone is obliged or able to attain to these heights; nevertheless, each one should correct his life and morals in his own measure in satisfaction to the divine justice: for it is to those who have endured voluntary sufferings in this life that the reward of virtue is vouchsafed. Moreover, when in the mystical body of Christ, which is the Church, all the members are united and flourish, it results, according to St. Paul, that the joy or pain of one member is shared by all the rest, so that if one of the brethren in Christ is suffering in mind or body the others come to his help and succor him as far as in them lies. The members are solicitous in regard of each other, and if one member suffer all the members suffer in sympathy, and if one member rejoice all the others rejoice also. But you are the body of Christ, members of one body (1 Cor 12:25-27). But in this illustration of charity, following the example of Christ, who in the immensity of his love gave up his life to redeem us from sin, paying himself the penalties incurred by others, in this is the great bond of perfection by which the faithful are closely united with the heavenly citizens and with God. Above all, acts of holy penance are so numerous and varied and extend over such a wide range, that each one may exercise them frequently with a cheerful and ready will without serious or painful effort.

12. And now, Venerable Brethren, your remarkable and exalted piety towards the most holy Mother of God, and your charity and solicitude for the Christian flock, are full of abundant promise: Our heart is full of desire for those wondrous fruits which, on many occasions, the devotion of Catholic people to Mary has brought forth; already we enjoy them deeply and abundantly in anticipation. At your exhortation and under your direction, therefore, the faithful, especially during this ensuing month, will assemble around the solemn altars of this august queen and most benign Mother, and weave and offer to her, like devoted children, the mystic garland so pleasing to her of the Rosary. All the privileges and indulgences we have herein before conceded are confirmed and ratified. [See encyclical *Supremi Apostolatus officio*; encyclical *Superiore anno*; decree *Inter plurimos*; encyclical *Quamquam pluries*.]

13. How grateful and magnificent a spectacle to see in the cities, and towns, and villages, on land and sea—wherever the Catholic faith has penetrated—many hundreds of thousands of pious people uniting their praises and prayers with one voice and heart at every moment of the day, saluting Mary, invoking Mary, hoping everything through Mary. Through her may all the faithful strive to obtain from her divine Son that the nations plunged in error may return to the Christian teaching and precepts, in which is the foundation of the public safety and the source of peace and true happiness. Through her may they steadfastly endeavor for that most desirable of all blessings, the restoration of the liberty of our Mother, the Church, and the tranquil possession of her rights—rights which have no other object than the careful direction of men's dearest interests, from the exercise of which individuals and nations have never suffered injury, but have derived, in all time, numerous and most precious benefits.

14. And for you, Venerable Brethren, through the intercession of the Queen of the Most Holy Rosary, we pray almighty God to grant you heavenly gifts, and greater and more abundant strength, and aid to accomplish the charge of your pastoral office. As a pledge of which we most lovingly bestow upon you and upon the clergy and people committed to your care, the Apostolic Benediction.

CHAPTER EIGHT

To Become Saints

It is not easy to become a saint. It requires sacrifice, dedication, heroic virtue, and, above all, a close relationship with Christ and a determination to follow his will, come what may. And yet sainthood—the product of a holy life—is what each of us is called to, despite the great challenge. For in holiness, we become who we were created and intended to be. The Dogmatic Constitution of the Catholic Church, *Lumen Gentium*, issued in 1964, explains this universal call to holiness:

> The Lord Jesus, the divine Teacher and Model of all perfection, preached holiness of life to each and every one of his disciples of every condition. He himself stands as the author and consumator of this holiness of life: "Be you therefore perfect, even as your heavenly Father is perfect." Indeed he sent the Holy Spirit upon all men that he might move them inwardly to love God with their whole heart and their whole soul, with all their mind and all their strength and that they might love each other as Christ loves

them. The followers of Christ are called by God, not
because of their works, but according to his own purpose and grace. They are justified in the Lord Jesus,
because in the baptism of faith they truly become
sons of God and sharers in the divine nature. In this
way they are really made holy. Then too, by God's
gift, they must hold on to and complete in their lives
this holiness they have received. They are warned by
the apostle to live "as becomes saints," and to put on
"as God's chosen ones, holy and beloved a heart of
mercy, kindness, humility, meekness, patience" (Col
3:12), and to possess the fruit of the Spirit in holiness. (40)

As in so many other aspects of our lives, the Rosary
shows us the way—this time to holiness. On All Saints Day
in 2003, Pope John Paul II called the Rosary "a simple and
accessible way for all to holiness, which is the vocation of
each baptized person." As Jesus instructed, we are to "be perfect, just as your heavenly Father is perfect" (Mt 5:48).

"The saints and blesseds of paradise remind us, as pilgrims on Earth, that prayer, above all, is our sustenance for
each day so that we never lose sight of our eternal destiny,"
St. John Paul said. "For many of them the Rosary ... was
the privileged instrument for their daily discourse with the
Lord. The Rosary led them to an ever more profound intimacy with Christ and with the Blessed Virgin."

In the history of the Church, many saints are known
for spreading devotion to Mary and the Rosary. St. Dominic, who is linked to the beginning and development of the
Rosary; St. Bartolo Longo, a former satanist who developed

a devotion to the Rosary; and, of course, St. John Paul, who gave the Church the great gift of the Mysteries of Light. But it was St. Louis de Montfort, born in France in 1673, who, in his extensive writing on the methodology behind praying the Rosary, identified the fruits of each mystery. St. John Paul II affirmed such a practice in *Rosarium Virginis Mariae*, writing, "It is worthwhile to note that the contemplation of the mysteries could better express their full spiritual fruitfulness if an effort were made to conclude each mystery with *a prayer for the fruits specific to that particular mystery*. In this way the Rosary would better express its connection with the Christian life" (35, emphasis in original).

In his "Methods for Saying the Rosary," St. Louis de Montfort suggested the following combinations of virtues with mysteries.

Joyful Mysteries

The Annunciation: Humility
The Visitation: Love of neighbor
The Nativity: Love of poverty and of the poor
The Presentation: Wisdom and purity of heart and body
The Finding of the Child Jesus in the Temple:
     Conversion of sinners, piety

Sorrowful Mysteries

The Agony in the Garden: For conformity to God's will
The Scourging at the Pillar: Grace to mortify our senses
     (purity)
The Crowning with Thorns: Deep contempt of the world
The Carrying of the Cross: Patience in carrying our cross

The Crucifixion: Great horror of sin, love of the cross, grace
   for a holy death

Glorious Mysteries

The Resurrection: For a lively faith
The Ascension: For a firm hope and a great longing for
   heaven
The Descent of the Holy Spirit: For holy wisdom that we
   may know, taste, practice, and share
The Assumption of Mary: For the gift of true devotion to
   her in order to live a good life and have a happy death
The Coronation of Mary as Queen of Heaven and Earth:
   For perseverance and an increase in virtue up to the
   moment of our death and thereafter the eternal crown
   that is prepared for us

Because the Luminous Mysteries weren't instituted until
well after St. Louis de Montfort's death, I have ventured to
suggest some options:

Luminous Mysteries

The Baptism of Jesus in the River Jordan: For obedience,
   vocation
The Wedding Feast at Cana: For a manifestation of God in
   the world through our actions, particularly in marriage
   and family life
The Proclamation of the Kingdom of God: For an
   evangelistic spirit
The Transfiguration of Jesus: For ongoing conversion to
   Christ

The Institution of the Eucharist: For a deeper love of and
reverence for the Blessed Sacrament

Through meditating upon and praying for these fruits of
the mysteries of the Rosary, we make the prayer ever more
relevant and meaningful to our everyday lives. We, too, are
able to more intentionally cultivate virtue, which helps lead
us to lives of holiness. Sainthood is not a thing of the past.
The need for holiness in the world is just as critical today as
it has been throughout the life of the Church. In his 2012
Angelus on All Saints Day, Pope Benedict XVI said, "In the
saints we see the victory of love over selfishness and death:
we see that following Christ leads to life, eternal life, and
gives meaning to the present, every moment that passes, because it is filled with love and hope."

Through prayer of the Rosary and virtuous living, the
hope is that, one day, we may be counted among their number.

Excerpts from Saints about the Rosary:
Pope St. John XXIII, St. Teresa of Calcutta,
St. Thérèse of Lisieux, St. Zélie Martin,
Blessed John Henry Newman, Pope St. John Paul II,
St. Louis de Montfort

Pope St. John XXIII

The Rosary, as an exercise of Christian piety among the
faithful of the Latin rite, who form a large part of the Catholic family, takes its place, for ecclesiastics, after holy Mass and
the Breviary, and for lay folk after their participation in the

sacraments. It is a devout form of union with God, and always has a most uplifting effect on the soul.

It is true that, in the case of some souls who have not been trained to rise above mere lip service, it may be recited as a monotonous succession of the three prayers: the Our Father, the Hail Mary, and the Gloria, arranged in the traditional order of fifteen decades. Even this, to be sure, is something. But, we must repeat, it is only the beginning or the external expression of trustful prayer, rather than the joyful flight of the soul in converse with God in the sublime and tender mysteries of his merciful love for all mankind.

The real substance of the well-meditated Rosary consists in a threefold chord which gives its vocal expression unity and cohesion, revealing in a vivid sequence the episodes which bind together the lives of Jesus and Mary, with reference to the various conditions of those who pray and the aspirations of the universal Church.

Every decade of Hail Marys has its own picture, and every picture has a threefold character which is always the same: *mystical contemplation, private reflection,* and *pious intention.*

First of all the *contemplation*, pure, clear and immediate, of every mystery, that is of those truths of the Faith which speak to us of the redeeming mission of Christ. As we contemplate we find ourselves in close communion of thought and feeling with the teaching and life of Jesus, Son of God and Son of Mary, who lived on this earth redeeming, teaching, sanctifying: in the silence of his hidden life, all prayer and work; in the sufferings of his blessed passion; in the triumph of his resurrection; in the glory of heaven, where he sits on the right hand of the Father, ever assisting and with his Holy Spirit giving life to the Church founded by him, which proceeds on its way throughout the centuries.

The second element is *reflection*, which out of the fullness of Christ's mysteries diffuses its bright radiance over the praying soul. Everyone finds in each mystery a good and proper teaching for himself, for his sanctification and for the conditions of his own life; under the constant guidance of the Holy Spirit, which from the depths of the soul in a state of grace "intercedes for us with sighs too deep for words" (Rom 8:26), everyone confronts his own life with the strength of the doctrine he has drawn from the depths of those same mysteries, and finds them of inexhaustible application to his own spiritual needs and to the needs of his daily life too.

Finally, there is the *intention*: that is intercession for persons, institutions, or necessities of a personal or social nature, which for a really active and pious Catholic forms part of his charity towards his neighbor, a charity which is diffused in our hearts as a living expression of our common sharing in the Mystical Body of Christ.

In this way the Rosary becomes a worldwide supplication of individual souls and of the immense community of the redeemed, who from all parts of the world meet in a single prayer, either in private petitions imploring graces for each one's personal needs, or in sharing in the immense and general chorus of the whole Church praying for the supreme interests of all mankind. The Church, as the divine Redeemer has ordained, lives amid the difficulties, conflicts, and storms of a social disorder that frequently becomes a frightening menace; but her eyes and her natural and supernatural energies are directed towards her supreme destiny of fulfilling the eternal purposes of God.

Source
Excerpt from the apostolic letter *The Religious Convention and the Rosary.*

St. Thérèse of Lisieux

How great is the power of prayer! One could call it a queen who has at each instant free access to the king and who is able to obtain whatever she asks. To be heard it is not necessary to read from a book some beautiful formula composed for the occasion. If this were the case, alas, I would have to be pitied! Outside the Divine Office, which I am very unworthy to recite, I do not have the courage to force myself to search out beautiful prayers in books. There are so many of them it really gives me a headache, and each prayer is more beautiful than the others. I cannot recite them all and not knowing which to choose, I do like children who do not know how to read, I say very simply to God what I wish to say, without composing beautiful sentences, and he always understands me. For me, prayer is an aspiration of the heart, it is a simple glance directed to heaven, it is a cry of gratitude and love in the midst of trial as well as joy; finally, it is something great, supernatural, which expands my soul and unites me to Jesus.

However, I would not want you to believe, dear Mother, that I recite without devotion the prayers said in common in the choir or the hermitages. On the contrary, I love very much these prayers in common, for Jesus has promised to be in the midst of those who gather together in his name. I feel then that the fervor of my Sisters makes up for my lack of fervor; but when alone (I am ashamed to admit it) the recitation of the Rosary is more difficult for me than the wearing of an instrument of penance. I feel I have said this so poorly! I force myself in vain to meditate on the mysteries of the Rosary; I don't succeed in fixing my mind on them. For a long time I was desolate about this lack of devotion, which astonished me, for I love the Blessed Virgin so much that it should be easy for me to recite in her honor prayers which are so pleasing to her. Now I am less desolate; I think that the Queen of Heaven, since she is my MOTHER, must see my good will and she is satisfied with it. Sometimes when my mind is in such aridity that it is impossible to draw forth one single thought to unite me with God, I very slowly recite an Our Father and then the angelic salutation ["Hail Mary, full of grace," etc.]; then these prayers give me great delight; they nourish my soul much more than if I had recited them precipitately a hundred times.

The Blessed Virgin shows me she is not displeased with me, for she never fails to protect me as soon as I invoke her. If some disturbance overtakes me, some embarrassment, I turn very quickly to her and as the most tender of Mothers she always takes care of my interests. How many times, when speaking to the novices, has it happened that I invoked her and felt the benefits of her motherly protection!

SOURCE
Story of a Soul, translated by Father John Clarke, OCD, published by ICS Publications.

St. Teresa of Calcutta (Mother Teresa)

Jim Castle was tired when he boarded his plane in Cincinnati that Friday night in 1981. All week long, the forty-five-year-old management consultant had put on a series of business workshops, and now he sank gratefully into an aisle seat, ready for the flight home to Kansas City.

More passengers entered ... the plane hummed with conversation, mixed with the sound of carry-on baggage being stowed.

Then, suddenly, people fell silent. The quiet moved slowly up the aisle like an invisible wake behind a boat. *What's happening?* wondered Jim, and craned his head to see. His mouth dropped open and he gasped.

Walking up the aisle were two nuns clad in simple white habits bordered in blue. At once he recognized the familiar face of one, the skin wrinkled, her eyes warmly intent—a face he'd seen in newscasts and on the cover of *Time*.

The two nuns halted, and Jim realized that his seat companion was going to be Mother Teresa.

As the last few passengers settled in, Mother Teresa and her companion, who sat next to the window, pulled out rosaries. Each decade of the beads was a different color, Jim noticed. The decades represented various areas of the world, Mother

Teresa told him later, and added, "I pray for the poor and dying on each continent."

The airplane taxied to the runway, and the two women began to pray, their voices a low murmur. Though Jim considered himself a ho-hum Catholic who went to church mostly out of habit, inexplicably he found himself joining in. By the time they murmured the final prayer, the plane had reached cruising altitude.

Mother Teresa turned toward him. For the first time in his life, Jim understood what people meant when they spoke of a person possessing an aura. As she gazed at him, a sense of peace filled him; he could no more see it than he could see the wind, but he felt it, just as surely as he felt a warm summer breeze. "Young man," she inquired, "do you say the Rosary often?" … he admitted, "No, not really."

She took his hand, while her eyes probed his. Then she smiled. "Well, you will now." And she dropped her rosary into his palm.

An hour later, Jim entered the Kansas City airport, where he was met by his wife, Ruth. "What in the world—?" began Ruth, as she noticed the rosary in his hand. They kissed and Jim described his encounter. Driving home, he said, "I feel as if I met a true sister of God."…

Nine months later, Jim and Ruth visited Connie, a longtime friend of theirs. Connie confessed that she'd been told she had ovarian cancer. "The doctor says it's a tough case, but I'm going to fight it. I won't give up!"

Jim clasped her hand. Then, after reaching into his pocket, he gently twined Mother Teresa's rosary around her fingers. He told her the story and said, "Keep it with you Connie.

It may help." Although Connie wasn't Catholic, her hand closed willingly around the small plastic beads. "Thank you," she whispered. "I hope I can return it."

More than a year passed before Jim saw Connie again. This time, face glowing, she hurried toward him and handed him the rosary. "I carried it with me all year," she said.... "I've had surgery and have been on chemotherapy, too. Last month, the doctors did second-look surgery, and the tumor's gone. Completely!" Her eyes met Jim's. "I knew it was time to give the rosary back."...

In the fall of 1987, Ruth's sister Liz fell into a deep depression after her divorce. She asked Jim if she could borrow the rosary, and when he sent it, she hung it over her bedpost in a small velvet bag.

"At night, I held on to it, just physically held on. I was so lonely and afraid," she admitted. "Yet when I gripped that rosary, I felt as if I held a loving hand." Gradually, Liz pulled her life together and she mailed the rosary back. "Someone else may need it," she said.

Then one night in 1988, a stranger telephoned Ruth. She'd heard about the rosary from a neighbor and asked if she could borrow it to take to the hospital where her mother lay in a coma. The family hoped the rosary might help their mother die peacefully.

A few days later, the woman returned the beads. "The nurses told me a coma patient can still hear," she said, "so I explained to my mother that I had Mother Teresa's rosary and that when I gave it to her, she could let go; it would be all right. Then I put the rosary in her hand. Right away, we saw her face relax! The lines smoothed out until she looked so peaceful. So young." The woman's voice caught.... "A few minutes later she was gone." Fervently, she gripped Ruth's hands. "Thank you."...

Jim's own life has changed after his unexpected meeting on the airplane.... When he realized Mother Teresa carries everything she owns in a small bag, Jim made an effort to simplify his own life. "I try to remember what really count—not money or titles or possessions, but the way we love others."

SOURCE
Unexpected Answers ("A Gift from the Woman in White," Chapter 24) by Barbara Bartocci, published by Our Sunday Visitor.

St. Zélie Martin

The daughter Marie recounts, "When she gets tired of having her head raised up [on a pillow?] we raise her up very slowly with the pillows until she is completely seated [upright]. But this never happens without incredible pain, because the least little movement makes her cry out in torment. And yet with what patience and acceptance does she put up with this sad illness! She never leaves her Rosary; she is always praying, in spite of her sufferings. We all admire her, because she has incomparable courage and energy. It has been fifteen days now, and she is still praying her Rosary, all the time on her knees at the feet of the Holy Virgin [statue] in her room, the one she loves so much. Seeing her so sick, I wanted to make her sit down, but it was useless."

SOURCE
Letter of July 8, 1877.

Blessed John Henry Newman

Now the great power of the Rosary lies in this, that it makes the Creed into a prayer; of course, the Creed is in some sense a prayer and a great act of homage to God; but the Rosary gives us the great truths of his life and death to meditate upon, and brings them nearer to our hearts. And so we contemplate all the great mysteries of his life and his birth in the manger; and so too the mysteries of his suffering and his glorified life. But even Christians, with all their knowledge of God, have usually more awe than love of him, and the special virtue of the Rosary lies in the special way in which it looks at these mysteries; for with all our thoughts of him are mingled thoughts of his Mother, and in the relations between Mother and Son we have set before us the Holy Family, the home in which God lived. Now the family is, even humanly considered, a sacred thing; how much more the family bound together by supernatural ties, and, above all, that in which God dwelt with his Blessed Mother.

This is what I should most wish you to remember in future years. For you will, all of you, have to go out into the world, and going out into the world means leaving home; and, my dear boys, you don't know what the world is now. You look forward to the time when you will go out into the world, and it seems to you very bright and full of promise. It is not wrong for you to look forward to that time; but most men who know the world find it a world of great trouble, and disappointments, and even misery. If it turns out so to you, seek a home in the Holy Family that you think about in the mysteries of the Rosary. Schoolboys know the difference between school and home. You often hear grown-up people say that the happiest time of their life was that passed at school, but when they were at school you know they had a happier time, which was when they went home; that shows there is a good in home which cannot be found elsewhere. So that even if the world should actually prove to be all that you now fancy it, if it should bring you all that you could wish, yet you ought to have in the Holy Family a home with a holiness and sweetness about it that cannot be found elsewhere.

SOURCE
Cardinal Newman had no official text for this short sermon delviered on October 5,1879. This is the text from a report in a local newspaper and written from notes taken at the time of the preaching. Present on the feast of the Holy Rosary, Cardinal Newman preached on the text: "They found Mary and Joseph, and the Infant lying in a manger" (Lk 2:16).

Pope St. John Paul II

The Rosary is my favorite prayer. A marvelous prayer! Marvelous in its simplicity and in its depth. In this prayer we repeat many times the words that the Virgin Mary heard from the archangel, and from her kinswoman Elizabeth. The whole Church joins in these words. It can be said that the Rosary is, in a certain way, a prayer-commentary on … the wonderful presence of the Mother of God in the mystery of Christ and the Church.

In fact, against the background of the words "Ave Maria" there pass before the eyes of the soul the main episodes in the life of Jesus Christ. They are composed altogether of the joyful, sorrowful and glorious mysteries, and they put us in living communion with Jesus through—we could say—his Mother's heart.

At the same time our heart can enclose in these decades of the Rosary all the facts that make up the life of the individual, the family, the nation, the Church, and mankind. Personal matters and those of one's neighbor, and particularly of those who are closest to us, who are dearest to us. Thus the simple prayer of the Rosary beats the rhythm of human life.

SOURCE
Angelus message, October 29, 1978.

St. Louis de Montfort

The Riches of Holiness Contained in the Prayers and Meditations of the Rosary

Never will anyone be able to understand the marvelous riches of sanctification which are contained in the prayers and mysteries of the holy Rosary. This meditation on the mysteries of the life and death of our Lord Jesus Christ is the source of the most wonderful fruits for those who make use of it.

Today people want things that strike and move them, that leave deep impressions on the soul. Now has there ever been anything in the history of the world more moving than the wonderful story of the life, death, and glory of our Savior which is contained in the holy Rosary? In the fifteen tableaux, the principal scenes or mysteries of his life unfold before our eyes. How could there be any more prayers more wonderful and sublime than the Lord's Prayer and the Ave of the angel? All our desires and all our needs are expressed in these two prayers.The meditation on the mysteries and prayers of the Rosary is the easiest of all prayers, because the diversity of the virtues of Our Lord and the different situations of his life which we study, refresh, and fortify our mind in a wonderful way and help us to avoid distractions. For the learned, these mysteries are the source of the most profound doctrine, while simple people find them a means of instruction well within their reach.

We need to learn this easy form of meditation before progressing to the highest state of contemplation. This is the view of St. Thomas Aquinas, and the advice that he gives when he says that, first of all, one must practice on a battlefield, as it were, by acquiring all the virtues of which we have the perfect model in the mysteries of the Rosary; for, says the learned Cajetan, that is the way we arrive at a really intimate union with God, since without that union contemplation is nothing but an illusion which can lead souls astray.

If only the Illuminists or Quietists of these days had followed this piece of advice, they would never have fallen so low or caused such scandals among spiritual people. To think that it is possible to say prayers that are finer and more beautiful than the Our Father and the Hail Mary is to fall prey to a strange illusion of the devil, for these heavenly prayers are the support, the strength, and the safeguard of our souls.

I admit it is not always necessary to say them as vocal prayers and that interior prayer is, in a sense, more perfect than vocal. But believe me, it is really dangerous, not to say fatal, to give up saying the Rosary of your own accord under the pretext of seeking a more perfect union with God. Sometimes a soul that is proud in a subtle way and who may have done everything that he can do interiorly to rise to the sublime heights of contemplation that the saints have reached may be deluded by the noonday devil into giving up his former devotions which are good enough for ordinary souls. He turns a deaf ear to the prayers and the greeting of an angel and even to the prayer which God has composed, put into practice, and commanded: Thus all you pray: Our Father. Having reached this point, such a soul drifts from illusion to illusion, and falls from precipice to precipice.

Believe me, dear brother of the Rosary Confraternity, if you genuinely wish to attain a high degree of prayer in all honesty and without falling into the illusions of the devil so common with those who practice mental prayer, say the whole Rosary every day, or at least five decades of it.

If you have already attained, by the grace of God, a high degree of prayer, keep up the practice of saying the holy Rosary if you wish to remain in that state and by it to grow in humility. For never will anyone who says his Rosary every day become a formal heretic or be led astray by the devil. This is a statement which I would sign with my blood.

On the other hand, if God in his infinite mercy draws you to himself as forcibly as he did some of the saints while saying the Rosary, make yourself passive in his hands and let yourself be drawn towards him. Let God work and praying you and let him say your Rosary in his way, and that will be sufficient for the day.

But if you are still in the state of active contemplation or the ordinary prayer of quietude, or the presence of God, affective prayer, you have even less reason for giving up the Rosary. Far from making you lose ground in mental prayer or stunting your spiritual growth, it will be a wonderful help to you. You will find it a real Jacob's ladder with fifteen rungs by which you will go from virtue to virtue and from light to light. Thus, without danger of being misled, you will easily arrive at the fullness of the age of Jesus Christ.

SOURCE
The Secret of the Rosary, "Twenty-Fifty Rose."

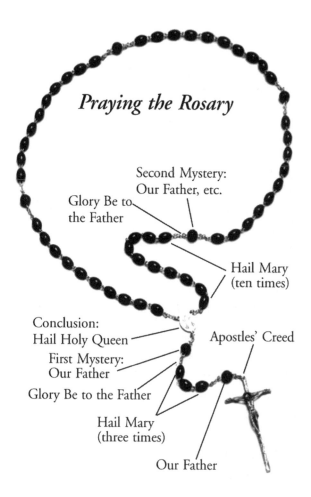

Praying the Rosary

Second Mystery:
Our Father, etc.

Glory Be to
the Father

Hail Mary
(ten times)

Conclusion:
Hail Holy Queen

Apostles' Creed

First Mystery:
Our Father

Glory Be to the Father

Hail Mary
(three times)

Our Father

Joyful Mysteries
traditionally prayed Mondays and Saturdays

The Annunciation
The Visitation
The Nativity
The Presentation in the Temple
The Finding in the Temple

Sorrowful Mysteries
traditionally prayed Tuesdays and Fridays

The Agony in the Garden
The Scourging at the Pillar
The Crowning with Thorns
The Carrying of the Cross
The Crucifixion

Luminous Mysteries
traditionally prayed Thursdays

The Baptism of Jesus in the River Jordan
The Wedding Feast at Cana
The Proclamation of the Kingdom of God
The Transfiguration of Jesus
The Institution of the Eucharist

Glorious Mysteries
traditionally prayed Wednesdays and Sundays

The Resurrection
The Ascension
The Descent of the Holy Spirit
The Assumption of Mary
The Coronation of Mary as Queen of Heaven and Earth

Prayers of the Rosary

Apostles' Creed

I believe in God, the Father almighty, Creator of heaven and earth, and in Jesus Christ, His only Son, our Lord, who was conceived by the Holy Spirit, born of the Virgin Mary, suffered under Pontius Pilate, was crucified, died and was buried; he descended into hell; on the third day he arose again from the dead; he ascended into heaven, and is seated at the right hand of God the Father almighty; from there he will come to judge the living and the dead. I believe in the Holy Spirit, the holy catholic Church, the communion of saints, the forgiveness of sins, the resurrection of the body, and life everlasting. Amen.

Our Father

Our Father, who art in heaven, hallowed be thy name. Thy kingdom come; thy will be done on earth as it is in heaven. Give us this day our daily bread, and forgive us our trespasses as we forgive those who trespass against us. And lead us not into temptation, but deliver us from evil. Amen.

Hail Mary

Hail Mary, full of grace, the Lord is with thee. Blessed art thou among women, and blest is the fruit of thy womb, Jesus. Holy Mary, Mother of God, pray for us sinners, now and at the hour of our death. Amen.

Glory Be
Glory be to the Father and to the Son and to the Holy Spirit, as it was in the beginning, is now and ever shall be, world without end. Amen.

Fátima Decade Prayer
O my Jesus, forgive us our sins, save us from the fires of hell. Lead all souls into heaven, especially those in most need of thy mercy.

Hail, Holy Queen
Hail, Holy Queen, Mother of Mercy, our life, our sweetness and our hope! To thee do we cry, poor banished children of Eve. To thee do we send up our sighs, mourning and weeping in this valley of tears. Turn, then, O most gracious Advocate, thine eyes of mercy toward us, and after this, our exile, show unto us the blessed fruit of thy womb, Jesus. O clement, O loving, O sweet Virgin Mary!

V. Pray for us, O Holy Mother of God.
R. That we may be made worthy of the promises of Christ.

Concluding Prayer
Let us pray. O God, whose only-begotten Son, by his life, death and resurrection, has purchased for us the rewards of eternal life, grant, we beseech Thee, that meditating upon these mysteries of the most holy Rosary of the Blessed Virgin Mary, we may imitate what they contain, and obtain what they promise, through the same Christ our Lord. Amen.

Acknowledgments

Much work has gone into the writing and compiling of this book. It could not have been done without the supportive team at Our Sunday Visitor, including the wisdom and fine editing of Jaymie Stuart Wolfe. A special thank you to Lori Pieper of the Pope John Paul I Association for permission to use her translation of the homily by Cardinal Albino Luciani. And many thanks to the men and women included in this work who were not afraid to share their deep love for and devotion to our Blessed Mother.

Acknowledgments for sources used in this book:

Chapter 1
"Is the Rosary Outdated?" from *A Passionate Adventure: Living the Catholic Faith Today*, translated with an introduction by Lori Pieper, OFS, preface by Justin Cardinal Rigali, published by Tau Cross Books and Media, New York, in 2014.

Chapter 1, 4, 6, 7, 8
Quotations from papal and other Vatican-generated documents are available on vatican.va and copyright © Libreria Editrice Vaticana.

Chapter 2
Excerpt from *The Worlds' First Love* by Archbishop Fulton J. Sheen (San Francisco: Ignatius Press, 1952, 2010), Chapter

8, "Roses and Prayers." www.ignatius.com. Used with permission.

Chapter 3

Excerpts from *All for Her*, Father Patrick Peyton, C.S.C., © Family Rosary, www.familyrosary.org.

Chapter 5

Exceprts from *The Rosary of Hiroshima* by Fr. Hubert F. Schiffer, SJ, 1953. Blue Army (World Apostolate of Fatima), Bluearmy.com.

Chapter 8

Excerpt from *Story of a Soul* by St. Thérèse of Lisieux, translated by John Clarke, O.C.D. Copyright © 1975, 1976, 1996 by Washington Province of Discalced Carmelites, ICS Publications, 2131 Lincoln Road, N.E., Washington, DC 20002-1199. www.icspublications.org.

"A Gift from the Woman in White" from *Unexpected Answers* © Barbara Bartocci. Published by Our Sunday Visitor.

Excerpt from *The Secret of the Rosary* by St. Louis de Montfort. Montfort Missionaries, www.montfortpublications.com.